QUESTIONS
JESUS ASKS

Israel Wayne

First printing: March 2015

ISBN: 978-0-89221-734-2
Library of Congress Number: 2015932311

Cover by Diana Bogardus

Unless otherwise noted, Scripture quotations are from the English Standard Version (ESV) of the Bible.

Please consider requesting that a copy of this volume be purchased by your local library system.

Printed in the United States of America

Please visit our website for other great titles:
www.newleafpress.net

For information regarding author interviews, please contact the publicity department at (870) 438-5288.

New Leaf Press
A Division of New Leaf Publishing Group
www.newleafpress.net

Table of Contents

Introduction — Was Jesus Omniscient?

My previous book, *Questions God Asks*, explored 19 questions asked by God to various individuals in the Old Testament. One of the intriguing concepts in that book is why an omniscient God, who knows the answer to every perceivable question, would ask questions.

It is obvious that the purpose of the question is not there for God's benefit but rather for the benefit of the person being asked. God wants that person to reconsider his or her assumptions, biases, preconceived ideas, and prejudices.

As I have endeavored to address this new subject of the *Questions Jesus Asks*, I have had to wrestle with a related question: "Was Jesus, in His incarnate state as a man on earth, omniscient?"

Did Jesus know everything that could possibly be known, or was His knowledge limited in some way because of His humanity? Let us explore these considerations.

Was Jesus Fully God?

Philippians 2:6 declares that Jesus was, in very nature, God. Colossians 2:9 says the fullness of God dwelt bodily in Jesus Christ. John 1, in referring to Jesus as "the Word," insists that the Word was with God and the Word *was God*! Hebrews 1:3 calls Jesus, "the radiance of the glory of God and the exact imprint of his nature." There are many other passages to which we could refer, but suffice it to say, Jesus was not partially God. He was completely, totally, and fully God, all the while being fully a human male. Theologians call this doctrine of the dilemma of Jesus' manhood and Godhood the

"Hypostatic Union" (see appendix). Jesus walked in fullness of all of the "Communicable Attributes" of God (see appendix).

Was Jesus Born Knowing Everything?

When Jesus was a little toddler, did He know not to touch a hot kettle? Did He know how to speak every language on earth? Did He automatically get the potty training thing from day one? The only personal glimpse we get into the childhood of Jesus, at age 12, shows Him in a learning posture.

> After three days they found him in the temple, sitting among the teachers, listening to them and asking them questions. And all who heard him were amazed at his understanding and his answers. And when his parents saw him, they were astonished. And his mother said to him, "Son, why have you treated us so? Behold, your father and I have been searching for you in great distress." And he said to them, "Why were you looking for me? Did you not know that I must be in my Father's house?" And they did not understand the saying that he spoke to them. And he went down with them and came to Nazareth and was submissive to them. And his mother treasured up all these things in her heart. And Jesus increased in wisdom and in stature and in favor with God and man (Luke 2:46–52).

Jesus' habit of asking questions began when He was quite young. In the very first place in the Scripture where it references Jesus speaking, He is asking questions. Why was He asking questions of the teachers of the law? Did He not understand certain concepts about the book He inspired? He certainly *did* understand who His Heavenly Father was, and that He had a unique call on His life. When Luke tells us that Jesus "increased" in wisdom, wouldn't that imply that He was born with a finite amount of wisdom? Omniscience, by definition, cannot be added to. "Increase" demonstrates that there was a growth, from a finite point to a more complete part.

The Book of Hebrews reiterates this concept of Jesus learning (as opposed to being born with infinite knowledge): "Although he was a son, he *learned* obedience through what he suffered" (Heb. 5:8, emphasis added).

Jesus Had Special Knowledge

There is no doubt that Jesus knew things that other people did not know, nor could have known.

In John 1:45–51, Philip found Nathanael and told him that he and his friends had found the long-awaited Messiah. Nathanael isn't buying it. He's like, "Dude? From Nazareth? For real?" But when he met Jesus, he quickly changed his mind. Jesus said, "Behold, an Israelite indeed, in whom there is no deceit." Nathanael asked, "How do you know me?" Jesus then told Nathanael that He saw him under the fig tree. That blew Nathanael's mind, and he declared, "You are the Son of God! You are the King of Israel!" Jesus assured him that he ain't seen nuthin' yet, and the best was yet to come.

In Matthew 17:24–27, Peter was asked if Jesus made a habit of paying the temple tax. Peter assured them that Jesus did pay the tax. Peter then entered the house where Jesus was staying, and Jesus raised the topic of paying tax. There was no way that Jesus could have known, in the natural, what they were discussing. This was special knowledge.

> Jesus saw [the lame man] lying there and knew that he had already been there a long time (John 5:6).

He knew that the disciples would abandon Him (Mark 14:27), Peter would deny Him (Matt. 26:34), and Judas would betray Him (John 13:27).

In Mark 9:33, the disciples had been arguing about who was the greatest in the Kingdom while they walked along the road, and Jesus seemed to hone in on it by asking them what they were talking about.

7

We are told that Jesus knew the hearts of people:

> But Jesus on his part did not entrust himself to them, because he knew all people and needed no one to bear witness about man, for he himself knew what was in man (John 2:24–25).

There are a number of times we are told that Jesus knew what people were thinking: Matthew 12:25, Mark 2:8, Luke 5:22, Luke 6:8.

> Jesus knew that they wanted to ask him, so he said to them, "Is this what you are asking yourselves, what I meant by saying, 'A little while and you will not see me, and again a little while and you will see me'?" (John 16:19).

This experience was enough for the disciples to become convinced of the omniscience of Jesus, believing that He knew all things.

> "Now we know that *you know all things* and do not need anyone to question you; this is why we believe that you came from God." Jesus answered them, "Do you now believe?" (John 16:30–31, emphasis added).

Jesus Was in Constant Communion with His Father

Some theologians insist that Jesus limited Himself, in His incarnate state, and did not make full access of the omniscience He had available to Him. Instead, He chose to rely on revelation He received from the Father.

> "All things have been handed over to me by my Father" (Luke 10:22).

> So Jesus said to them, "Truly, truly, I say to you, the Son can do nothing of his own accord, but only what he sees the Father doing. For whatever the Father does, that the Son does likewise" (John 5:19).

"I can do nothing on my own. As I hear, I judge, and my judgment is just, because I seek not my own will but the will of him who sent me" (John 5:30).

"I do nothing on my own authority, but speak just as the Father taught me" (John 8:28).

"For I have not spoken on my own authority, but the Father who sent me has himself given me a commandment — what to say and what to speak" (John 12:49).

While on the earth, Jesus did only the works that His Father told Him to do, and only spoke the words that His Father told him to speak. He was totally reliant upon His Father for wisdom and direction in His ministry (thus providing a model for us to follow).

Did Jesus Limit Some Aspects of His Divinity?

While it is incomprehensible for us to consider a fully-God person lacking some of the attributes of God-ness, we know there are aspects of His divinity that Jesus laid down when He took on human flesh.

Jesus was not omnipresent in His human state. He wasn't physically in every place at the same time. And while Jesus is eternal, His human form on earth was finite.

"For this reason the Father loves me, because I lay down my life that I may take it up again. No one takes it from me, but I lay it down of my own accord. I have authority to lay it down, and I have authority to take it up again. This charge I have received from my Father" (John 10:17–18).

God cannot die. God is not biological. God is Spirit (John 4:24), and yet Jesus' physical body died. That doesn't mean that Jesus was any less divine, nor any less eternal in this fulfillment of God's will.

Have this mind among yourselves, which is yours in Christ Jesus, who, though he was in the form of God, did

9

not count equality with God a thing to be grasped, but emptied himself, by taking the form of a servant, being born in the likeness of men. And being found in human form, he humbled himself by becoming obedient to the point of death, even death on a cross (Phil. 2:5–8).

It is important for us to understand that in any way that Jesus was limited by His humanity, it was totally and completely voluntary. He was not weakened in any way that He did not choose to be.

Was Jesus' Knowledge Limited?

In Luke 8:45–46, some argue that Jesus was truly puzzled when He was touched by the woman with the issue of blood:

> And Jesus said, "Who was it that touched me?" When all denied it, Peter said, "Master, the crowds surround you and are pressing in on you!" But Jesus said, "Someone touched me, for I perceive that power has gone out from me."

Some believe that Jesus knew who had touched Him, but was wanting to draw the woman out of the crowd into a public confession of her need.

Others point to occasions where the Bible records that Jesus was surprised or astonished by a statement or a set of events (Matt. 8:10, Mark 6:6, Luke 7:9). It could even be said that Jesus was surprised that His parents were surprised that He was in the temple. "Why were you looking for me? Did you not know that I must be in my Father's house?" (Luke 2:49).

Some cite Jesus' cry on the Cross, "My God, my God, why have you forsaken me?" (Matt. 27:46), as a genuine expression of bewilderment.

To each of the passages cited above, there are explanations on the other side that would insist that Jesus is *not* asking these questions out of a lack of infinite knowledge but rather for the benefit of His hearers.

However, there is at least one place where Jesus clearly expresses that His knowledge is limited:

"But concerning that day or that hour, no one knows, not even the angels in heaven, nor the Son, but only the Father" (Mark 13:32).

So Why Did Jesus Ask Questions?

While Bible scholars debate the extent of knowledge to which Jesus may or may not have limited Himself during the 33 years of His humanity, we do know that Jesus had such a close, intimate relationship with the Father that He knew anything He needed to know to fulfill His earthly ministry. He knew the inclination of people's hearts. Many times it is demonstrated that He knew their thoughts.

I personally believe that Jesus' motivation in asking questions was usually very similar to the reasons we explored in *Questions God Asks*. He isn't asking the questions for His own personal benefit but rather on behalf of the person being asked. Jesus was full of love and compassion for people. His questions penetrate the heart and probe our deepest motives.

I love the fact that whenever others sought to trap Him with a question, Jesus would almost inevitably avoid answering and respond with a question of His own (which usually left His opponents speechless).

Because these questions of Jesus have been preserved for us in the Scripture, I believe they are there for our benefit as well. What does Jesus want us to consider about our assumptions, our prejudices, and our innermost thoughts and secrets? I invite you to join with me on this journey of discovery as we seek to find our answers through the *Questions Jesus Asks*.

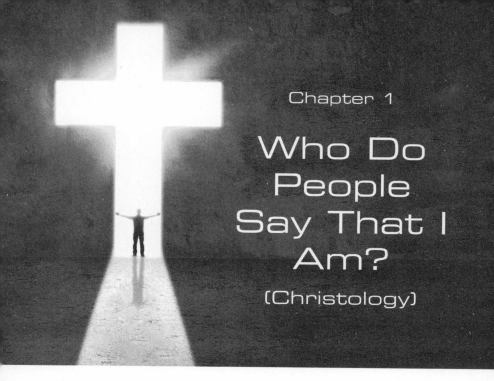

Chapter 1

Who Do People Say That I Am?

(Christology)

When I was a teenager, I started a unique radio show. It was called, "Teen to Teen," and it featured random "man-on-the-street" interviews I conducted with other teens. I would ask them questions to learn their views on various matters. It was actually a lead-in for evangelism. I would go to malls, skating parties, arcades (okay, teenagers: don't ask . . . I know, I'm old!), and other places where teens hung out. I found that people will open up to a person with a microphone in his hand and engage in conversations they might not otherwise.

The show never became a broadcast success, but I learned that people have opinions about everything: divorce, drugs, suicide, relationships, religion . . . you name it! I learned a lot about the beliefs and values of my generation from asking questions and listening to their answers.

Who Is Jesus?

If you were to do investigative interviews with average Americans, you would likely receive many different responses to the question, "Who was/is Jesus?"

If you were to ask the famous atheist evangelist Richard Dawkins, you would hear this:

> Jesus was a great moral teacher. Somebody as intelligent as Jesus would have been an atheist if He had known what we know today.[1]

The late atheist author Christopher Hitchens denied Jesus' existence:

> Jesus of Nazareth is not a figure in history . . . there is no firm evidence that He existed.[2]

Famous atheist Bertrand Russell wrote:

> I now want to say a few words upon a topic which I often think is not quite sufficiently dealt with by Rationalists, and that is the question whether Christ was the best and the wisest of men. It is generally taken for granted that we should all agree that that was so. I do not myself. I think that there are a good many points upon which I agree with Christ a great deal more than the professing Christians do. I do not know that I could go with Him all the way, but I could go with Him much further than most professing Christians can.[3]

Deepak Chopra, a new age guru, says, "I see Christ as a state of consciousness that we can all aspire to."[4]

---

1. http://www.theguardian.com/science/video/2011/oct/24/richard-dawkins-video-interview.
2. For a TV video of Hitchens at Politics and Prose Bookstore, Washington, DC, May 10, 2007, see http://fora.tv/2007/05/10/Christopher_Hitchens_at_Politics_and_Prose/.
3. From his 1927 essay, "Why I Am Not a Christian," http://users.drew.edu/~jlenz/whynot.html.
4. http://transcripts.cnn.com/TRANSCRIPTS/0412/24/lkl.01.html.

Former Bible college graduate and current agnostic professor Bart Ehrman has this opinion:

> The Christians did not invent Jesus. They invented the idea that the Messiah had to be crucified . . . Whether we like it or not, Jesus certainly existed.[5]

Atheist author Sam Harris has this cynical view of Jesus:

> Jesus Christ, a carpenter by trade, was born of a virgin, ritually murdered as a scapegoat for the collective sins of his species, and then resurrected from death after an interval of three days. He promptly ascended, bodily, to "heaven" — where, for two millennia, he has eavesdropped upon (and, on occasion, even answered) the simultaneous prayers of billions of beleaguered human beings. Not content to maintain this numinous arrangement indefinitely, this invisible carpenter will one day return to earth to judge humanity for its sexual indiscretions and skeptical doubts, at which time he will grant immortality to anyone who has had the good fortune to be convinced, on Mother's knee, that this baffling litany of miracles is the most important series of truth claims ever revealed about the cosmos. Every other member of our species, past and present, from Cleopatra to Einstein, no matter what his or her terrestrial accomplishments, will (probably) be consigned to a fiery hell for all eternity.[6]

One world-renown religious leader declares Jesus to be merely another human being:

> I think of Jesus as a human being, a historical person later understood as the Son of God. I relate to Him as a

---

5. http://www.huffingtonpost.com/bart-d-ehrman/did-jesus-exist_b_1349544.html.

6. http://www.project-reason.org/archive/item/what_should_science_dosam_harris_v_philip_ball/.

natural Jesus, an extraordinary human being, one of the few who have become universal teachers.[7]

What do the majority of contemporary Americans believe about who Jesus is?

A 2013 Harris poll stated that most Americans believe Jesus is God or the Son of God (68 percent, down from 72 percent in 2005), He was born of a virgin (57 percent, down from 60 percent), and He rose again from the dead (65 percent, down from 70 percent).[8]

Who Do People Say That I Am?

Now when Jesus came into the district of Caesarea Philippi, He asked His disciples, "Who do people say that the Son of Man is?" And they said, "Some say John the Baptist, others say Elijah, and others Jeremiah or one of the prophets" (Matt. 16:13–14, see also Mark 8:27–28).

Now it happened that as he was praying alone, the disciples were with him. And He asked them, "Who do the crowds say that I am?" And they answered, "John the Baptist. But others say, Elijah, and others, that one of the prophets of old has risen" (Luke 9:18–19).

Why is Jesus concerned about what people think of Him? Is this a brief moment of insecurity? Is Jesus taking a poll to assess His popularity, or to discern the effectiveness of His recent public relations campaign?

Didn't Jesus already know what people thought about Him? Was this question for His benefit? Or was it for the benefit of the

---

7. Fr. Laurence Freeman (a monk of the Olivetan Benedictine Congregation of Monte Oliveto Maggiore, and Director of The World Community for Christian Meditation), http://dalailama.com/news/post/900-dialogue-between-his-holi-ness-the-dalai-lama-and-fr-laurence-freeman-about-the-teacher-and-disciple-in-sarnath-varanasi.

8. "Americans' Belief in God, Miracles and Heaven Declines," The Harris Poll® #97, December 16, 2013, by Larry Shannon-Missal, Harris Poll Research Manager, www.harrisinteractive.com

disciples? If for the disciples, what did Jesus want them to consider or understand?

It is evident from the passage that the disciples had heard the identity of Jesus discussed by people in the area. They knew the current opinions about Jesus. Apparently, the view of the masses was generally favorable. They put Him in the category of godly prophets and leaders they respected. That was a good thing, right?

Why Should We Care What People Think about Jesus?

As Christians, our mandate is to share the love and truth of who Jesus actually is with the world around us. An important part of evangelism and defending the faith (Christian apologetics) is knowing what people in our culture currently believe about who Jesus is.

Was He just a "good moral teacher"? Was He merely a Jewish carpenter who lived in the first century? Is He just another spiritual option in a pantheon of gods and deities? Knowing the preconceived ideas and notions of those around us will help us to converse with them more intelligently and effectively.

I'm sure that this was much of Jesus' motivation in asking His disciples what their neighbors believed about Him. They could not be effective witnesses for Him (as they would later be called to do) unless they understood what people already believed to be true about Him.

Who Do *You* Say That I Am?

Jesus didn't end His inquiry with the opinions of the masses. He then turned it closer to home and honed in on the personal beliefs of His own followers.

> "But who do *you* say that I am?" (Matt. 16:15, emphasis added).

Jesus gave His disciples an opportunity to verbalize what they believed.

What Do Christians in America Believe about Jesus?

From my point of view, the future of Christianity in the West hinges on whether or not the youth embrace the Christian faith.

According to Christian researcher George Barna, the majority of churched youth have very unorthodox views about Jesus.

Although 87 percent of teens believe Jesus was a real person who lived on earth, and 78 percent believe He was born to a virgin, nearly half (46 percent) believe He committed sins, and more than half (51 percent) say Jesus died but never rose from the dead.[9] The vast majority (65 percent) either believe or suspect there is "no way to tell which religion is true."[10]

One survey of churched youth who self-identify as Christians revealed that only 24 percent would strongly and consistently affirm belief that Jesus is God.[11]

These professing Christian youth, who regularly attend various denominational churches, were asked to affirm the following four statements:

1. The Bible is completely trustworthy in what it says about Jesus.
2. Jesus Is God.
3. Jesus physically lived, died, and came back to life.
4. Jesus is the only way to heaven.

Sadly, only 9 percent of churched youth would consistently express confidence in these doctrines.[12]

This lack of confidence in the truth of the Bible and the historical reliability of the deity of Christ has resulted in a tsunami of young people abandoning the church. Ken Ham, in his church-shaking book *Already Gone*, reveals that two-thirds of all Christian youth

---

9. George Barna, *Third Millennium Teens: Research on the Minds, Hearts and Souls of America's Teenagers* (Ventura, CA: Barna Research Group, Ltd., 1999), p. 48.
10. Josh McDowell and Bob Hostetler, *Right From Wrong* (Nashville, TN: Word Publishing, 1994), p. 263.
11. Mike Nappa, *The Jesus Survey* (Grand Rapids, MI: Baker Books, 2012), p. 34.
12. Ibid., p. 86, 88.

who are currently attending church, are "already gone" in their hearts.[13] They plan to leave the church as soon as they can, with no plans to return.

You Are the Messiah!

When Jesus asked His disciples who they thought Jesus was, the Apostle Peter, who was never at a loss for words, was the first to pipe up:

> "You are the Christ, the Son of the living God" (Matt. 16:16).

Jesus was pleased with the answer.

> Jesus replied, "Blessed are you, Simon son of Jonah, for this was not revealed to you by flesh and blood, but by my Father in heaven" (Matt. 16:17; NIV).

Jesus affirms Peter's declaration, but then, as if to demonstrate that He was in no way trying to win a popularity contest, "He strictly charged the disciples to tell no one that he was the Christ" (Matt. 16:20).

As a side note, the account of this event recorded in Mark's gospel does not record the positive words that Jesus spoke to Peter, but only the rebuke a few verses later. Peter was very close friends with John Mark, even calling him "my son" (1 Pet. 5:13) and most likely related these accounts to him personally. The fact that Peter included the rebuke, but not the commendation, probably reflects the humility of Peter after his transformation at Pentecost.

Who Do You Say Jesus Is?

This question is not merely for the 12 disciples of Jesus. It resonates in our hearts today. Who do you believe Jesus is/was? I believe this is the most important question we can ever answer.

I love C.S. Lewis's (1898–1963) response to this question:

13. Ken Ham and Britt Beemer, with Todd Hillard, *Already Gone* (Green Forest, AR: Master Books, 2009), p. 22.

I am trying here to prevent anyone saying the really foolish thing that people often say about Him: I'm ready to accept Jesus as a great moral teacher, but I don't accept his claim to be God. That is the one thing we must not say. A man who was merely a man and said the sort of things Jesus said would not be a great moral teacher. He would either be a lunatic — on the level with the man who says he is a poached egg — or else he would be the Devil of Hell. You must make your choice. Either this man was, and is, the Son of God, or else a madman or something worse. You can shut him up for a fool, you can spit at him and kill him as a demon or you can fall at his feet and call him Lord and God, but let us not come with any patronizing nonsense about his being a great human teacher. He has not left that open to us. He did not intend to. . . . Now it seems to me obvious that He was neither a lunatic nor a fiend: and consequently, however strange or terrifying or unlikely it may seem, I have to accept the view that He was and is God.[14]

It is my sincere hope that you will not respond to this question lightly. If Jesus' claims are true, then eternity is in the balance.

---

14. C.S. Lewis, *Mere Christianity* (London: Collins, 1952), p. 54–56 (in all editions, this is Bk. II, Ch. 3, "The Shocking Alternative").

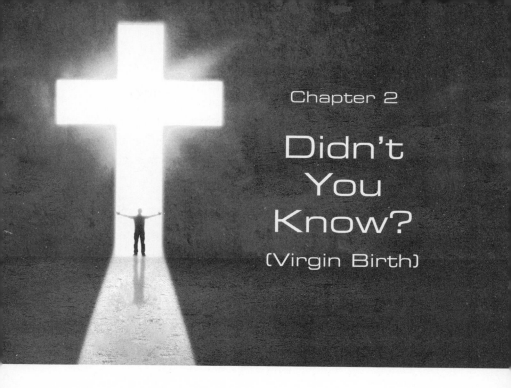

Chapter 2

Didn't You Know?

(Virgin Birth)

My oldest son is named, "Benjamin." The name is Hebrew in origin (*Binyamin*), meaning "son of my right hand," or "son of my days." I think it's a great name, and it reflects my relationship with my son. In the ancient Hebrew culture, men were often identified as being the son of their father. The name "Ben" in Hebrew means "son." You may have seen the epic film, *Ben Hur*, starring Charlton Heston, based on the book by Lew Wallace. His name means "Son of Hur."

This tradition of connecting the son to his father goes deep in the biblical tradition. When Jesus was growing up in Nazareth, He likely would have been known around town as "Yeshua Ben Yossef," or "Jesus, son of Joseph."

Indeed, in Matthew 13:55, we hear His neighbors saying of Him, "Is not this the carpenter's son?" Respect and honor of one's parents, and father in particular, was of supreme importance within the biblical culture.

Who Is Your Father?

> Now his parents went to Jerusalem every year at the
> Feast of the Passover. And when he was twelve years old,
> they went up according to custom. And when the feast was
> ended, as they were returning, the boy Jesus stayed behind
> in Jerusalem. His parents did not know it, but suppos-
> ing him to be in the group they went a day's journey, but
> then they began to search for him among their relatives
> and acquaintances, and when they did not find him, they
> returned to Jerusalem, searching for him. After three days
> they found him in the temple, sitting among the teach-
> ers, listening to them and asking them questions. And all
> who heard him were amazed at his understanding and his
> answers. And when his parents saw him, they were aston-
> ished. And his mother said to him, "Son, why have you
> treated us so? Behold, your father and I have been search-
> ing for you in great distress." And he said to them, "Why
> were you looking for me? Did you not know that I must
> be in my Father's house?" And they did not understand the
> saying that he spoke to them. And he went down with them
> and came to Nazareth and was submissive to them. And his
> mother treasured up all these things in her heart. And Jesus
> increased in wisdom and in stature and in favor with God
> and man" (Luke 2:41–52).

In the very first passage of Scripture that describes Jesus talking, we
find Him engaged in a practice He would continue for His entire
life: asking questions. He is questioning the teachers of law and
responds to His parents' questions with a question (again, a life-
long pattern).

This entire narrative baffles me from the perspective of a parent.
Instead of leaving Jerusalem with His parents, He stays behind. I
mean, it sounds exactly like something I would have done at that

age, but as a father, it isn't what I would imagine Jesus doing. What kind of a question is, "Why were you looking for me?" Does Jesus not understand anything about parenting? Keeping track of your child is pretty integral to the entire process of being a parent. Clearly, His family was very concerned while He was missing and searches for Him for three days before they find Him safe in the temple. Yet there is a very important distinction being made in this account of Jesus' life between the earthly and the divine.

Then there is the "Didn't you know . . . ?" part and the "Father's house" bit. How could Joseph and Mary be expected to have any clue where to find Jesus? It all has to do with who Jesus was and what was prophesied about Him.

Jesus' response to His parents seems dismissive and borderline rude, particularly in light of the culture of that day, where children were not commonly allowed the kind of forceful entrance into the world of adults as they are today. Jesus actually seems to be distancing Himself from His earthly heritage.

Rather than embracing and promoting His lineage, as any good Hebrew boy would, by referring to "My Father's house," Jesus is emphasizing His spiritual, rather than physical, identity. He continues this throughout His life by referring to Himself with the term "Son of Man," a Messianic term He draws from the prophetic Book of Daniel. However, because the text describes the submissive posture of Jesus toward His parents, we know that He was not acting in rebellion but rather in obedience to the call of God that He was beginning to sense in His young life.

Born of a Virgin

More than anyone in the room at that moment, His mother, Mary, knew the truth of who Jesus' Father truly was (you can read the account of Jesus' conception and birth in Luke 1). She had been warned in a prophecy at that same temple, only 12 years earlier, that her son's mission would "pierce her heart." I'm sure she must have left the temple that day with extremely mixed emotions, marveling at the promise regarding her son, yet having the maternal desire to protect Him from the pain that would soon come as He embraced His emerging destiny as a man.

In the history of mankind, there has never been a suspension of the regular course of human reproduction. Even with modern bio-medical engineering, there are still limits to what science is capable of achieving. The claim that a person was not only born to a virgin, but was conceived by the very Spirit of God, is an unheard of proposition. The logical "Law of the Excluded Middle" insists that there is no middle ground on this issue. Jesus couldn't have been "kind of" born to a virgin. This is an all-or-nothing truth claim.

Despite the assertions of some popular "emergent church" teachers who posit the contrary, this is not a theologically insignificant issue. One author suggested that if we were to somehow discover (through some kind of DNA test, etc.) that Jesus' real father was a human, and that He was born through natural means (like everyone else), there would still be many valid reasons to embrace Christianity. But this is not so. Everything hinges on this core doctrine.

Dr. G. Campbell Morgan (1863–1945), the pastor of Westminster Chapel in London, said this of the supernatural doctrine of the virgin birth:

> On the question of the birth of Jesus, of course I should feel almost angry with anyone who used the word "illegitimate." The whole matter is unique, separate, lonely. Yes, there is no questions but that Joseph married Mary directly he knew that she was with child by the Holy Spirit; but as the record tells us, he lived in continence during the whole period until after the birth of Jesus. I cannot see why you, or anyone else, should say that the whole thing is unbelievable. The only reason why it is unbelievable must be found in a conception of God which limits Him to action within

laws which man has so far discovered. That, to me, is an entirely unbelievable position.[1]

Cult leaders through the centuries have claimed to be Jesus, or have claimed to have been born through a miraculous virgin birth, but none have substantiated the claims through miracles, living a sinless life, and then predicting their death and resurrection (and then fulfilling the promise). Jesus stands alone in this distinction.

What makes Christianity distinct from every other religion is that Jesus did not merely claim to be a prophet who spoke for God. He claimed to be God Himself! It is His claim to have God as His Father (and to be co-eternal with Him) that sets Him apart from every other religious leader throughout history.

Did Jesus Claim to Be God?

> They answered him, "Abraham is our father." Jesus said to them, "If you were Abraham's children, you would be doing the works Abraham did, but now you seek to kill me, a man who has told you the truth that I heard from God. This is not what Abraham did. You are doing the works your father did." They said to him, "We were not born of sexual immorality. We have one Father — even God." Jesus said to them, "If God were your Father, you would love me, for I came from God and I am here. I came not of my own accord, but he sent me. Why do you not understand what I say? It is because you cannot bear to hear my word" (John 8:39–43).

Ever been in a conversation and you suddenly realize you aren't truly communicating with the other person? Jesus asks a question here to point out that genuine conversation isn't transpiring here. What is happening is that His opponents have their minds made up, and they are in attack mode. They aren't genuinely trying to learn from Jesus about His teachings or His claims. They are forming the arguments in their minds even as He is speaking.

---

1. http://www.gcampbellmorgan.com/twhf16.pdf.

Not content to engage the discussion on the level of issues that are on the table, Jesus' opponents go for a low blow. The result to an *ad hominem* personal attack of the worst sort. They accuse Jesus, very publicly, of that scandal that has probably been whispered in neighboring villages for years. Jesus' young mother "had to get married," because she had "jumped the gun" and had become pregnant before her wedding day. Rumor had it that Joseph wasn't even the real father. Jesus was, in the minds of His critics, not the high and mighty religious pontiff that He thought He was, but rather He was the product of a sinful and disgraceful act that should have been punished by stoning. Who was He to be telling the truly religious people what God expected? The arrogance!

Not to be deterred from His position, Jesus shot back a scathing rebuke of His own.

> "You are of your father the devil, and your will is to do your father's desires. He was a murderer from the beginning and does not stand in the truth, because there is no truth in him. When he lies, he speaks out of his own character, for he is a liar and the father of lies. But because I tell the truth, you do not believe me. Which one of you convicts me of sin? If I tell the truth, why do you not believe me? Whoever is of God hears the words of God. The reason why you do not hear them is that you are not of God" (John 8:44–47).

In order for Jesus to be convicted of sin, He would have to be accused by two or three witnesses of a definite violation of the Law (Deut. 17:6). Jesus exposed that the true reason they were angry, and actually wanted to kill Him, is because they were being motivated by their spiritual father, who was not God but the devil. The issue of spiritual paternity was key to this exchange.

Jesus ended the dialogue in John 8 by making a truly remarkable claim. He referred to Himself, using the covenant name by which God revealed Himself to Moses at the burning bush: "I AM."

"Truly, truly, I say to you, before Abraham was, I am."
So they picked up stones to throw at him, but Jesus hid
himself and went out of the temple (John 8:58–59).

In case you wonder if the religious leaders missed the claim to
deity, their response of trying to stone Him for blasphemy leaves no
doubt. Jesus believed He was God.

Christian apologist Ravi Zacharias shares this:

> I have often referenced the quote by the talk show host,
> Larry King, in his response to a particular question: "If you
> could select any one person across all of history to interview,
> who would it be?" Mr. King's answer was that he would like
> to interview Jesus Christ. When the questioner followed
> with, "And what would you like to ask him?" King replied,
> "I would like to ask him if he was indeed virgin-born. The
> answer to that question would define history for me." The
> first time I requested permission through a common friend
> to use this quote of his, he sent word saying, "And tell him
> I was not being facetious." I believe him. Who would not
> like to interview Jesus Christ?"[2]

Is the Virgin Birth Important?

In contrast to the postmodern church leaders of our day, the church
father Irenaeus (A.D. 130–202) believed that failing to believe in the
Virgin Birth would keep someone from eternal life.

> But again, those who assert that He was simply a mere
> man, begotten by Joseph, remaining in the bondage of the
> old disobedience, are in a state of death having been not
> as yet joined to the Word of God the Father, nor receiving
> liberty through the Son, as He does Himself declare: "If the
> Son shall make you free, ye shall be free indeed." But, being

---

2. http://www.rzim.org/a-slice-of-infinity/questioning-christ/, posted by Ravi
Zacharias on February 24, 2011.

ignorant of Him who from the Virgin is Emmanuel, they are deprived of His gift, which is eternal life; and not receiving the incorruptible Word, they remain in mortal flesh, and are debtors to death, not obtaining the antidote of life.[3]

Dr. Albert Mohler, president of the Southern Baptist Theological Seminary, takes this well-balanced view:

> Must one believe in the Virgin Birth to be a Christian? This is not a hard question to answer. It is conceivable that someone might come to Christ and trust Christ as Savior without yet learning that the Bible teaches that Jesus was born of a virgin. A new believer is not yet aware of the full structure of Christian truth. The real question is this: Can a Christian, once aware of the Bible's teaching, reject the Virgin Birth? The answer must be no.[4]

As true Christians, we believe the entire teaching of the Bible, without equivocation. We believe in the miraculous. We do not believe every wild and mystical claim made by deranged humans throughout time, but we do believe that God chose to become a man and live among us in the person of Jesus of Nazareth. Jesus' question, "Didn't you know I must be in My Father's house?" lies at the very core of our theology. If Christ was not virgin born, then He was not God, nor would He have been able to live a sinless life, nor be a perfect sacrifice for our sins, nor would He have been able to rise again, nor would He have ascended into heaven, sat at the right hand of the Father, nor would He be able to return again in glory, judgment, and honor in the future. This belief, affirmed in all of the Early Church creeds and confessions, is at the very core of the gospel, and we dare not abandon this fundamental tenet amidst the skepticism of our age.

---

3. Ante-Nicene Fathers, (Against Heresies III:19:1), compiled by Phillip Schaaf.
4. http://www.albertmohler.com/2011/12/14/must-we-believe-in-the-virgin-birth. This essay was originally posted December 8, 2006.

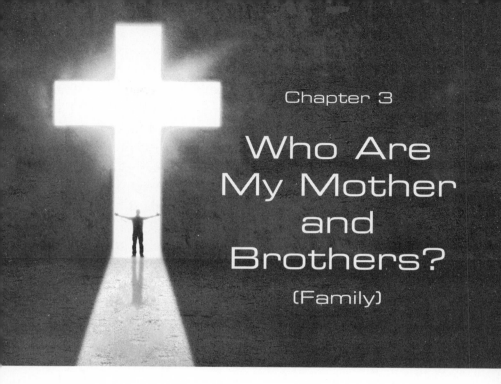

Chapter 3

Who Are My Mother and Brothers?

(Family)

When I was a little tyke, I loved to hear stories read to me. That was probably because it took me so long to learn how to read myself. Many of my early books were heart-warming and entertaining, expanding my imagination and whisking me away to other amazing realms. Then some of them, which I'm sure were meant to be enjoyable, I actually found a bit disturbing.

Dr. Seuss's books were like that for me. I mean, I'd seen green ham before, but there was nothing appealing about it at all! And many of the characters had issues too. Especially the Yink, who liked to drink pink ink. There was something not quite right about that guy. I'm just sayin'!

One of these creepy stories, that I think was supposed to be endearing, was called, "Are You My Mother?" It was, as best as I remember, about an unborn baby bird in an egg, whose mother left the nest to go to Walmart to get groceries. While she was gone, the baby bird popped out from the egg in her nest. I'm guessing, as happens today, there were probably 26 registers in the store, but only two of them were open, so by the time the mom got back home, the baby bird had grown up and gone looking for her. (The actual details may have become fuzzy over time, but that's okay. My version is better anyway.)

Because the little bird had no self-identity, he would approach perfect strangers: a cat, a chicken, a dog, a cow, even machines like boats, planes, and excavators. Eventually he is reunited with his real mother, and they all live happily ever after.

It's all in good fun, right? I don't know. It seems to me that very few things in life are more traumatic to a five-year-old than the thought of being alone in the world, totally abandoned by your parents, not knowing who you are, and not knowing where you belong. (Okay, I admit to being overly analytical even as a munchkin!)

Who Are You?

The customary introduction in the Bible for men was something like this: "And these are the sons of Benjamin: Sallu the son of Meshullam, son of Joed, son of Pedaiah, son of Kolaiah, son of Maaseiah, son of Ithiel, son of Jeshaiah" (Neh. 11:7).

You knew who a man was because of his relationship to his father. You were the son of your dad. Lineage and heritage tell us who we are and where we came from. Even Jesus experienced this in His adult years: "Is not this the carpenter's son? Is not his mother called Mary? And are not his brothers James and Joseph and Simon and Judas?" (Matt. 13:55).

The world chose to view Jesus' identity through a natural lens. Jesus, on the other hand, knew that His actual lineage was quite different. When His parents found Him in the temple at age 12, after looking for Him for three days, Jesus responded, in His first words recorded in Scripture with a question: "And he said to them, 'Why were you looking for me? Did you not know that I must be in my Father's house?' " (Luke 2:49).

Jesus viewed His lineage as being, not of this world, but rather from eternity. I don't think it was that Jesus didn't value and appreciate His earthly parents, but He recognized that there was a realm that transcends this brief mortal span.

All in the Family

According to Mark 6:3 and Matthew 13:55–56, Jesus' brothers were named James, Joseph (Joses), Judas (Jude), and Simon. We are told that He had sisters as well. Jesus was the older, and His younger siblings were all natural-born children from the marriage between Joseph and Mary. It is probably safe to assume that Joseph died sometime after the scenario at the temple when Jesus was 12 and before Jesus began His public ministry. There is no mention of him in the New Testament, and he was clearly no longer living when Jesus died, thus necessitating Jesus (as the oldest son) to turn the care of his mother over to John the disciple (see John 19:26–27).

While Jesus' family is mentioned in Scripture, His familial relations are minimized in comparison to His teaching and healing ministry. There is so much more mention of His interactions with His disciples than His own siblings. Part of the reason for this may be revealed in John 7:5 where we are told that Jesus' own brothers did not believe in Him. So while He had that natural brotherly connection they shared from growing up together, they did not agree on the most important things: common faith, vision, and belief.

This situation came to a head when Jesus' family showed up one day to try to exercise an intervention on Him.

> Then he went home, and the crowd gathered again, so that they could not even eat. And when his family heard it, they went out to seize him, for they were saying, "He is out of his mind" (Mark 3:20–21).

It's one thing to have your family not share your values, but it's a completely different level to have your family think you are a loony case because of your beliefs. We seldom think of the myriad of ways in which Jesus experienced the everyday difficulties and struggles we ourselves face. Whoever would consider that Jesus was not necessarily relationally close with His own family? We know that all of us have had difficult family relationships at some point, but the Son of God? Yes, Jesus experienced that as well, and He did so for our sake.

> Therefore he had to be made like his brothers in every respect, so that he might become a merciful and faithful high priest in the service of God, to make propitiation for the sins of the people (Heb. 2:17).

In an attempt to rescue Jesus, His family appeared, unannounced, and expected Jesus to drop what He was doing and get on board with their agenda. Jesus, however, was not going to be deterred from His mission.

> And his mother and his brothers came, and standing outside they sent to him and called him. And a crowd was sitting around him, and they said to him, "Your mother and your brothers are outside, seeking you." And he answered them, "Who are my mother and my brothers?" And looking about at those who sat around him, he said, "Here are my mother and my brothers! For whoever does the will of God, he is my brother and sister and mother" (Mark 3:31–35).

Twenty years after the event at the temple with Jesus' parents, we see the scene basically replayed. Jesus' family came looking for Him, but they had their own agenda in mind, not His. When He was 12, Jesus identified His father not as Joseph, the carpenter of Nazareth, but instead, the Lord of the universe. In this case, He did not consider His true mother and brothers to be His biological family but, rather, His disciples. It is those who share the Kingdom agenda who are greatly esteemed by Jesus.

Jesus Is Our Brother

When you and I enter into this relationship with Jesus, as His disciples, we enter into a unique kind of adoption into His spiritual family.

For it was fitting that he, for whom and by whom all things exist, in bringing many sons to glory, should make the founder of their salvation perfect through suffering. For he who sanctifies and those who are sanctified all have one source. That is why he is not ashamed to call them brothers, saying, "I will tell of your name to my brothers; in the midst of the congregation I will sing your praise" (Heb. 2:10–12).

Jesus not only called the 12 disciples His brothers, but He calls us brothers and sisters as well.

We Are Family

J.C. Ryle (1816–1900), in his sermon "The Family of God," said:

Membership in "the family of God" does not depend on any earthly connection. It does not come by natural birth, but by new birth. Ministers cannot impart it to their hearers. Parents cannot give it to their children. You may be born in the godliest family in the land, and enjoy the sweetest fellowship of grace that any Church can supply, and yet never belong to the family of God. To belong to it you must be born again. No one but the Holy Spirit can make you a living member of this family. It is His special function and prerogative to bring into the true Church all those who will be saved. Those who are born again are born, "not of natural descent, nor of human decision or a husband's will, but born of God" [John 1:13].[1]

When we enter into God's family, we suddenly get a whole new batch of siblings. I've always believed the understated truth of the saying, "You can pick your friends, but you can't pick your family." That is so true! It's true in God's family as well.

We don't always feel the most comfortable with other Christians. Some of them are a bit odd and quirky. Some are still spiritually

---

1. www.SermonIndex.net.

immature and lacking in sanctification. But like them or not, you've got to learn to love them. They're your new kin! These are the people you are going to spend eternity with in heaven, so you might as well try to learn to get along while we're here together.

I have some family who are also my spiritual family. That is a double blessing! I have some biological relatives who are not walking with the Lord. I pray for them, that they will turn. As long as there is life, there is hope!

In Jesus' case, the Resurrection and Pentecost seemed to do something amazing and transformative in the hearts of His own family members. Two of our epistles, James and Jude, were written by Jesus' brothers! His brother James became an Apostle and was a leader of the church in Jerusalem. What a blessing to know that the message of the risen Christ finally made an impact on Jesus' own brothers. May it make a transformation in the hearts of all those we love as well!

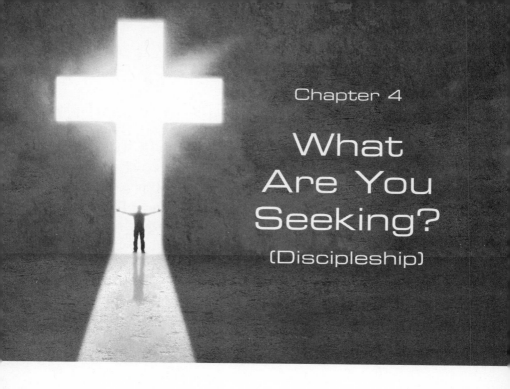

Chapter 4

What Are You Seeking?

(Discipleship)

When I was speaking in Japan some years ago, I took a day to be a tourist and visited several Buddhist temples. One of the most memorable was Kinkaku-ji (or "Rokuon-ji"), the "Temple of the Golden Pavilion" in Kyoto. It dates back to A.D. 1397. The structure is stunning as its gold color gleams brightly in the resplendent sunshine. The building is visited by thousands of spiritual pilgrims from around the world as they seek to pay homage to the founder of the Buddhist religion, Gautama (also called, "Siddharta") Buddha, whose ashes are reported to be stored in the pavilion.

Gautama was a fascinating historical character. He lived from approximately 563 to 480 B.C. The Eastern culture into which he was born was heavily influenced by Hinduism and reincarnation. Even though he had an affluent childhood, he felt there had to be something more to life than the ceaseless cycle of death, karma, and rebirth. At the age of 29, he left his wife and son and went on a spiritual pilgrimage. His goal was to find enlightenment. The nickname, Buddha, means the "awakened one" or "enlightened one."

Through yoga and meditation, Gautama believed that he finally reached a higher spiritual plane called "Nirvana." Nirvana is a term that means, literally, "to extinguish" or "blow out." The idea is that when you reach this higher level of consciousness, you get to die and just stay dead. You can escape from the tyranny of coming back in various forms, in a meaningless march of determined existence.

Gautama was seeking freedom from the tyranny of fate and bad karma. Many of his followers down through the centuries have sought solace and wisdom from his teachings, as well as made pilgrimages to various sacred sites.

We see similar devotion in searching for answers among modern adherents to Hinduism and Islam, as well as scores of other smaller religions. Humans are inherently spiritual, and the search for meaning and purpose is endemic to the human heart.

What Are You Seeking?

In Jesus' day, the Jewish people were searching for the Messiah. They awaited a deliverer who could break the bands of tyranny imposed by the *Pax Romana* ("Roman Peace"), and restore Israel to her former glory. There was a kind of apocalyptic tenor in the air at the time that Jesus began His earthly ministry. The Essenes in the Qumran community (the group who had copied and preserved the "Dead Sea Scrolls") had extensive literature indicating that they believed they were living in the "last days," and very soon the Messiah(s) would arrive.

It is in that context that John the Baptist, a man who would have surely fit the part of an end-time action film, began preaching and baptizing on the banks of the Jordan River.

> The next day, again John was standing with two of his disciples, and he looked at Jesus as he walked by and said, "Behold, the Lamb of God!" The two disciples heard him

say this, and they followed Jesus. Jesus turned and saw them following and said to them, "What are you seeking?" (John 1:35–38).

Immediately, Jesus sought to identify why these men wanted to follow Him. It is interesting to note that Jesus understood the fascination people had with John and knew why people were attracted to him.

"What did you go out into the wilderness to see? A reed shaken by the wind? What then did you go out to see? A man dressed in soft clothing? Behold, those who wear soft clothing are in kings' houses. What then did you go out to see? A prophet? Yes, I tell you, and more than a prophet" (Matt. 11:7–9).

There is a sense in which a lot of people will flock to anyone who is a bit *avant garde*. Throughout time, religious zealots, even those who are uniquely bizarre and esoteric, attract seekers. There are those who get tired of the *status quo* and are ready for something a little radical and out of the box. Jesus asked questions to identify the expectations of His would-be followers.

The Homeless King

And they said to him, "Rabbi' (which means Teacher), "where are you staying?" He said to them, "Come and you will see." So they came and saw where he was staying, and they stayed with him that day, for it was about the tenth hour" (John 1:38–39).

If the disciples followed Jesus out of a desire for mansions, luxury, and prosperity, they were going to be disappointed from the get-go.

And a scribe came up and said to him, "Teacher, I will follow you wherever you go." And Jesus said to him, "Foxes have holes, and birds of the air have nests, but the Son of Man has nowhere to lay his head" (Matt. 8:19–20).

Throughout His earthly ministry, Jesus put no emphasis on amassing earthly wealth. In fact, He often warned against it.

"Do not lay up for yourselves treasures on earth, where moth and rust destroy and where thieves break in and steal, but lay up for yourselves treasures in heaven, where neither moth nor rust destroys and where thieves do not break in and steal. For where your treasure is, there your heart will be also. . . . No one can serve two masters, for either he will hate the one and love the other, or he will be devoted to the one and despise the other. You cannot serve God and money" (Matt. 6:19–24).

Instead of material possessions, Jesus' focus was on preaching the gospel to the poor (Luke 4:18) and ministering to the people. His ministry was not about building up a physical empire but rather about giving Himself away for others.

We Have Found the Messiah!

Thankfully, the disciples were not put off by the meager accommodations and simple lifestyle of Jesus. In fact, in a very short period of time, they had become convinced that Jesus was not merely another interesting teacher or prophet, but He was the One prophesied by the Scriptures to save the people of Israel.

One of the two who heard John speak and followed Jesus was Andrew, Simon Peter's brother. He first found his own brother Simon and said to him, "We have found the Messiah" (which means Christ) (John 1:40–41).

John the Baptist's proclamation of Jesus as "the Lamb of God" was not merely a declaration of Jesus as the Messiah, but it was also a description of His call.

Charles Spurgeon (1834–1892), the great British preacher, put it this way:

There was nothing of greater wonder ever seen than that God Himself should provide the Lamb for the burnt offering, that He should provide His only Son out of His very bosom, that He should give the delight of His heart to die for us. Well may we behold this great wonder. Angels admire and marvel at this mystery of godliness, God manifest in the flesh; they have never left off wondering and adoring the grace of God that gave Jesus to be the Sacrifice for guilty men. Behold and wonder, never leave off wondering; tell it as a wonder, think of it as a wonder, sing of it as a wonder at this glorious Lamb of God.[1]

Seeker-Sensitive?

In the 1990s we experienced the "seeker-sensitive" movement in the evangelical church. The goal was to connect with those who were looking for spirituality, and provide a welcoming, non-threatening atmosphere where they wouldn't feel judged or uncomfortable.

Jesus' methods differed greatly from the postmodern, "seeker-friendly" model. Rather than trying to make people feel at ease, it seems that Jesus went out of His way to unsettle others. His approach was the direct opposite of what today's marketing experts would have advised.

"The Son of Man must suffer many things and be rejected by the elders and chief priests and scribes, and be killed, and on the third day be raised." And he said to all, "If anyone would come after me, let him deny himself and take up his cross daily and follow me. For whoever would save his life will lose it, but whoever loses his life for my sake will save it. For what does it profit a man if he gains the whole world and loses or forfeits himself? For whoever

---

1. Charles Spurgeon, www.Spurgeon.org, A Sermon (No. 2329) intended for reading on Lord's Day, October 8, 1893, delivered by C.H. Spurgeon at the Metropolitan Tabernacle, Newington, England, on Lord's-day evening, August 25, 1889.

is ashamed of me and of my words, of him will the Son of Man be ashamed when he comes in his glory and the glory of the Father and of the holy angels" (Luke 9:21–26).

The question Jesus asked is relevant to us today. Who or what are we seeking? Fame? Power? Wealth? Pleasure? Knowledge? Comfort? Security? Acceptance? Jesus knows our heart's desire, and it is His will that we desire to follow Him above all else.

Dietrich Bonhoeffer (1906–1945), in his epic book *The Cost of Discipleship,* describes the call of the disciple this way:

> The call goes forth, and is at once followed by the response of obedience. The response of the disciples is an act of obedience, not a confession of faith in Jesus. How could the call immediately evoke obedience? . . . For the simple reason that the cause behind the immediate following of call by response is Jesus Christ himself. It is Jesus who calls, and because it is Jesus, (the disciple) follows at once. . . . Jesus summons men to follow him not as a teacher or a pattern of the good life, but as the Christ, the Son of God. . . . Not a word of praise is given to the disciple for his decision for Christ. We are not expected to contemplate the disciple, but only he who calls, and his absolute authority. . . . There is no road to faith or discipleship, no other road — only obedience to the call of Jesus.[2]

Who Is Jesus Seeking?

> For the eyes of the LORD run to and fro throughout the whole earth, to give strong support to those whose heart is blameless toward him" (2 Chron. 16:9).

> "And I sought for a man among them who should build up the wall and stand in the breach before me for the

---

2. Dietrich Bonhoeffer, *The Cost of Discipleship* (New York, NY: Collier Books, Macmillan Publishing Company, First Edition published in 1949), p. 61–62.

land, that I should not destroy it, but I found none" (Ezek. 22:30).

"But this is the one to whom I will look: he who is humble and contrite in spirit and trembles at my word" (Isa. 66:2).

Before there were "seekers" there was the One who seeks. The Jesus who asks us what we are seeking, is also searching, looking for those who are lost.

For the Son of Man came to seek and to save the lost (Luke 19:10).

And the master said to the servant, "Go out to the highways and hedges and compel people to come in, that my house may be filled" (Luke 14:23).

"Those whom I love, I reprove and discipline, so be zealous and repent. Behold, I stand at the door and knock. If anyone hears my voice and opens the door, I will come in to him and eat with him, and he with me" (Rev. 3:19–20).

The Savior is inviting us to "come and see," to join Him as a fully committed follower. Whether your need is to begin that journey for the first time, or to return from a season of straying from His lead, I hope you will choose to follow this Messiah, this deliverer, this suffering Lamb, for He alone has the words of eternal life (John 6:68). The end of the Christian's journey isn't nothingness, as Gautama envisioned, but rather a life without end with Jesus in the true "Golden Temple."

And I saw no temple in the city, for its temple is the Lord God the Almighty and the Lamb. And the city has no need of sun or moon to shine on it, for the glory of God gives it light, and its lamp is the Lamb. By its light will the nations walk, and the kings of the earth will bring their glory into it, and its gates will never be shut by day — and there will be no night there. They will bring into it the glory and the honor of the nations. But nothing unclean will ever enter it, nor anyone who does what is detestable or false, but only those who are written in the Lamb's book of life (Rev. 21:22–27).

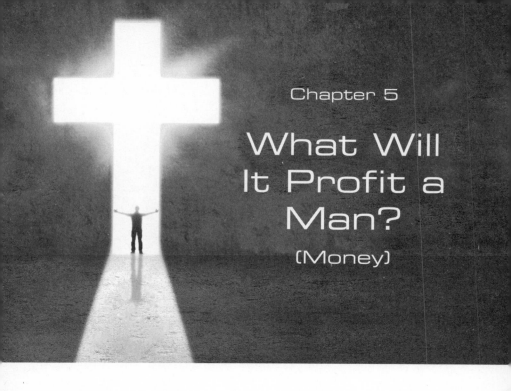

Chapter 5

What Will It Profit a Man?

(Money)

The late financial consultant and author Larry Burkett used to make the radical claim that you can tell what someone values, and even what they worship, by looking at two things: their checkbook and their calendar. Your time and resources are the two main aspects of your life. Your talents are appropriated through these two channels.

Many Christians claim that their top priorities in life are God, their family, and church. However, when you look at their week, they spend 19 minutes a day in interaction with their children, spend 10 minutes in a morning devotional, and put five dollars in the offering plate for the missionary who speaks at their church. These same parents spend two and a half hours watching television every night, and think nothing of dropping hundreds of dollars on a new entertainment system or several thousand dollars on a summer vacation. The way we spend our lives, through our time and resources, reveals who we really are and what we value.

Some people think that money is a bad thing, or a necessary evil, so they think that Christians should avoid both studying the topic and seeking to gain wealth. Deuteronomy 8:18 tells us that God gives us the ability to produce wealth. Far from being a secular topic that Jesus avoided, Jesus spoke more about money than anyone in the Bible. He spoke about money more than He talked about heaven or hell. The Bible includes 2,350 verses in Scripture dealing with money and possessions.[1]

Investing in Eternity

R.G. LeTourneau (1888–1969) was a Christian man who manufactured large earth-moving equipment during the first half of the 20th century. Despite being in business during the Great Depression, LeTourneau was highly successful, and he became a millionaire. Rather than hoarding the money for himself, he was committed to investing in the work of the Kingdom. In fact, he eventually began to give away 90 percent of his income to the Lord's work.

In an interview with Robert Ripley (of "Ripley's Believe it or Not" fame), LeTourneau said, "To date, $10,000,000 has been given to the Lord's share. . . . You see, I don't feel that my brain made this money. I believe the Lord made it possible for me to make it, and I'm only returning to God what belongs to Him. My motto is not how much of my money do I give to God, but how much of God's money do I keep for myself?"[2]

How could someone give away 90 percent of his income, and still be a millionaire? In his book, *Movers of Men and Mountains*, LeTourneau explained, "I shovel the money out, and God shovels it back in — and God has a larger shovel than I do."[3]

1. http://www.compasseuropartners.eu/wp-content/uploads/2013/03/2350-verses-on-money.pdf.
2. R.G. LeTourneau, *God Runs My Business* (Grand Rapids, MI: Fleming H. Revell Company, 1941), p. 126.
3. Quoted in *Business by the Book: The Complete Guide of Biblical Principles for the Workplace*, by Larry Burkett (Nashville, TN: Thomas Nelson Publishers, 1998), p. 238.

Everything Belongs to God

If you were raised in church, or have been in one for any length of time, you have probably heard this teaching: "Ten percent of everything you earn belongs to God, and 90 percent of it belongs to you. So make sure that you give God His share."

This idea, based on the tithe found in the Old Testament, is misleading and inaccurate. First of all, in the Old Testament, there wasn't just one tithe, there were three.

The three different types are as follows:

1. The Levitical, or sacred tithe (Num. 18: 21, 24)
2. The tithe of the feasts (Deut. 14:22–27)
3. The tithe for the poor (Deut. 14:28–29)

It is not my intent to do a complete study of the tithe here (although I encourage you to do that independently), but rather to point out that God's people actually gave a lot more than 10 percent of their annual income. Most scholars agree that the total combined required tithe of people in the Old Testament would have been an average of 23.3 percent of their annual income.

Even in the Old Testament, the concept of God owning 10 percent, or even 23.3 percent, is fallacious. Everything belongs to God. "For 'the earth is the Lord's, and the fullness thereof' " (1 Cor. 10:26). Please see the endnote for a more detailed study on this fact.[4]

Stewardship

In the New Testament, there is no specific percentage required for us to give. Now, lest you draw a sigh of relief and suppose that this gets you off of your responsibility to give, remember that Jesus didn't come to abolish the law, but to fulfill it. As with all of His teachings in the Sermon on the Mount, Jesus insisted, "For I tell you, unless

4. Passages that indicate that God owns everything: Gen. 14:19, 14:22; Exod. 9:29, 19:5; Deut. 10:14; 1 Chron. 29:11, 14–16; Job 41:11; Ps. 24:1, 50:12, 82:8, 89:11, 95:4–5, 104:24.

your righteousness exceeds that of the scribes and Pharisees, you will never enter the kingdom of heaven" (Matt. 5:20).

I believe the parable of the stewards, in Matthew 25:14–30, gives us a good narrative of how we are to view finances. God owns everything, and He apportions different amounts of money for us to manage on His behalf.

> One who is faithful in a very little is also faithful in much, and one who is dishonest in a very little is also dishonest in much. If then you have not been faithful in the unrighteous wealth, who will entrust to you the true riches? And if you have not been faithful in that which is another's, who will give you that which is your own? (Luke 16:10–12).

Look at it this way — suppose you and I have a boss, and we are financial managers for him. He gives you a million dollars to invest for his company, and he gives me ten dollars. Which of us is more wealthy, you or me? Well, technically, we're both broke! We have nothing. It is our boss who is rich, not us.

In this context, consider this teaching of Jesus on wealth:

> And Jesus said to his disciples, "Truly, I say to you, only with difficulty will a rich person enter the kingdom of heaven. Again I tell you, it is easier for a camel to go through the eye of a needle than for a rich person to enter the kingdom of God." When the disciples heard this, they were greatly astonished, saying, "Who then can be saved?" But Jesus looked at them and said, "With man this is impossible, but with God all things are possible" (Matt. 19:23–26).

Can a billionaire enter the Kingdom of God? I'm going to suggest it depends on who really owns that wealth. If I am managing a billion dollars for someone else, that is a tremendous trust and responsibility, but I'm still poor. That money is not mine; I just manage it. I'm going to suggest that the person who will not enter the Kingdom is the one who believes that what they have belongs to them.

God Owns My Business

Another businessman who gave large percentages of his income to the work of the Lord was Stanley Tam, owner of United Plastics.

On January 15, 1955, Dr. R. Stanley Tam, founder of the United States Plastic Corporation (a company he started with $37.00), made a bold move to legally turn his entire business over to God. Mr. Tam placed 100 percent of the ownership of USPC into a foundation whose purpose is to establish churches in third-world countries. By 2014, the nonprofit had donated over $140,000,000 to the work of Christian evangelism, had planted over 300 churches worldwide, and had seen over 140,000 decisions to follow Christ. His story is told in the book *God Owns My Business*.

Money Is a Wonderful Servant, but It Is a Brutal Master

Jesus asked this poignant question:

> "For what will it profit a man if he gains the whole world and forfeits his soul? Or what shall a man give in return for his soul?" (Matt. 16:26).

Money is a means, not an end. Are we using money to love and serve God, and love and serve other people, or to love and serve ourselves?

> "No servant can serve two masters, for either he will hate the one and love the other, or he will be devoted to the one and despise the other. You cannot serve God and money." The Pharisees, who were lovers of money, heard all these things, and they ridiculed him (Luke 16:13–14).

Giving

Jesus presupposes that believers will give money to help those in need.

> "Thus, when you give to the needy, sound no trumpet before you, as the hypocrites do in the synagogues and in

the streets, that they may be praised by others. Truly, I say to you, they have received their reward. But when you give to the needy, do not let your left hand know what your right hand is doing, so that your giving may be in secret. And your Father who sees in secret will reward you" (Matt. 6:2-4).

You'll notice that Jesus doesn't say, "*If* you give . . ." but, rather, "*when* you give. . . ." Giving generously and joyfully is a sign of the work of the Holy Spirit in our lives.

"Do not lay up for yourselves treasures on earth, where moth and rust destroy and where thieves break in and steal, but lay up for yourselves treasures in heaven, where neither moth nor rust destroys and where thieves do not break in and steal. For where your treasure is, there your heart will be also" (Matt. 6:19–20).

The Apostle Paul spoke of the "grace of giving."

"But as you excel in everything — in faith, in speech, in knowledge, in all earnestness, and in our love for you — see that you excel in this act of grace also" (2 Cor. 8:7).

Greed vs. Contentment

Someone once reportedly asked America's first billionaire, John D. Rockefeller Sr., "How much money is enough money?" He replied, "Just a little bit more."

Jesus had almost no physical possessions. He owned no home and had to borrow a donkey to ride into Jerusalem. When His taxes were due, He sent Peter fishing. He left us an example of how to be free from greed.

Keep your life free from love of money, and be content with what you have, for he has said, "I will never leave you nor forsake you" (Heb. 13:5).

But godliness with contentment is great gain, for we brought nothing into the world, and we cannot take anything out of the world. But if we have food and clothing, with these we will be content. But those who desire to be rich fall into temptation, into a snare, into many senseless and harmful desires that plunge people into ruin and destruction. For the love of money is a root of all kinds of evils. It is through this craving that some have wandered away from the faith and pierced themselves with many pangs (1 Tim. 6:6–10).

Unlike the prosperity preachers of our day who live opulently, and talk about how God wants you to be rich (because you deserve it), Jesus lived a life of contentment and used money to do the work of the Father and to bless and serve others.

Trust

Worry over financial issues is one of the main factors in marital conflict. It is the cause of major stress-induced health problems and lots of sleepless nights. Jesus commands us to avoid this.

"Therefore I tell you, do not be anxious about your life, what you will eat or what you will drink, nor about your body, what you will put on. Is not life more than food, and the body more than clothing? Look at the birds of the air: they neither sow nor reap nor gather into barns, and yet your heavenly Father feeds them. Are you not of more value than they?" (Matt. 6:25–26).

We have no reason to fear. Our Father in heaven knows our needs before we even ask Him.

George Müller of Bristol, England (1805–1898), was a man who had phenomenal trust in God and His ability to provide. During his life he started orphanages and cared for over 10,000 orphans. He also established 117 Christian schools to provide a Christian education for over 120,000 children. His life is a great example of not only trusting God to miraculously provide funds for their needs, but also of careful stewardship, ensuring that none of the money God provided would be wasted or used in a frivolous manner. I strongly encourage you to read a few biographies on his amazing life.

What Will It Profit You?

One day, each of us, rich or poor, will die and stand before our Maker. How did we invest our lives? How well did we steward the resources God entrusted to us? Were we more consumed with material possessions or eternal souls? We bring nothing into this life and we will take nothing physical with us into eternity. As the missionary to Africa, C.T. Studd (1860–1931), once said, "Only one life, t'will soon be past. Only what's done for Christ will last."[5]

The great evangelist John Wesley (1703–1791), in his sermon in 1744, "The Use of Money," outlined these principles (my paraphrase):

1. Earn all you can (through honest and diligent labor).
2. Save all you can.
3. Waste nothing.
4. Give all you can.

May these wise principles be our guiding light as we invest in what truly matters: eternal rewards.

---

5. https://www.goodreads.com/quotes/549103-only-one-life-twill-soon-be-past-only-what-s-done.

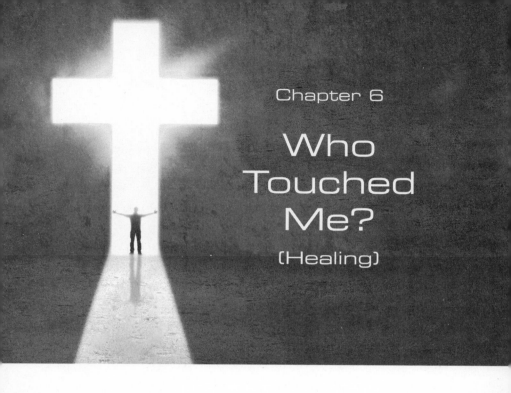

Chapter 6

Who Touched Me?

(Healing)

The doctrine of healing has always been a difficult one for me. When I was very young, I was raised in a conservative Fundamentalist church that held dogmatically to a theology called "cessationism." In layman's terms, at least as my church related it to this issue, it basically means that if you are sick, you'd better go to a doctor and take some medicine, because that is the only way God is going to heal you nowadays. All of the miraculous healings you read about in the Book of Acts ended in Acts, and now we rely on science and technology, not supernatural intervention. We were encouraged to pray, of course, but we prayed for the doctors to have skill and wisdom, and the medicine to work quickly. Our church was very reactionary against the concept of "faith healing" and especially "faith healers."

When I was six, my dad made a radical departure from that into a charismatic church. This church believed in supernatural healing of the sick, and believed that we could do greater miracles than Jesus and the Apostles. The tension between these two positions was obviously one that was hard to reconcile. At that young age, I wasn't sure what to think, but I decided to keep an open mind.

I'll never forget a young lady at the charismatic church named Shari (not her real name). She was one of the most joyful people I ever saw. I found that to be ironic, especially given the fact that she had cerebral palsy, and could barely walk, even with special crutches.

Be Healed!

In the early 1980s, there were quite a few itinerant "healers" who would make the rounds of various churches, doing special meetings and inviting the sick and lame to be healed. Every time one of these healers came around, Shari's mom and brother would take her to the meetings for prayer. In some of these meetings, people who looked pretty healthy went forward to receive prayer for things like migraines or stomach aches. Many of them claimed to be healed. It was revealed by national investigative news agencies that some of those "faith healers" were really charlatans, who used deceptive methods to hoodwink their audiences.

Shari wasn't in a position to fake her condition. If she got healed, there would be no doubt about it. I saw Shari go forward dozens of times, and dozens of times I saw her go home just as disabled as before. In some cases, screeners refused to even let her on stage, but led her to a back room for prayer. One of the most memorable occasions was when a so-called faith healer grabbed Shari's crutches and hurled them across the stage. When she began to stagger without her supports, he informed the audience that she was just "drunk in the spirit." I went back to being a cessationist.

In spite of all of the foolishness, and all of the disappointment that Shari experienced, she never lost hope that God would heal her. She never lost her smile. She never lost her joy. I admired her. I wished I could be like her in that respect.

The Tension Continues

I remained a cessationist on the issue of healing until one day when I was an early teen. I saw, with my own eyes, my baby sister instantly and miraculously healed from a life-threatening sickness. I couldn't explain it, but I also couldn't explain it away. It's an amazing story; I'd love to tell you over coffee someday.

Today, I don't think I fit into any tidy little category on this issue. I believe that God is sovereign and that He can heal anyone, from anything, any time He wants to, through means that we may not expect. At the same time, I don't send money to people I see on television who have prayed over handkerchiefs, or bottled up "holy healing water" from the Dead Sea. I try my best to have genuine faith in God, even in the midst of my inherent skepticism about shady hucksters.

I find that there are a lot of Christians like me. We pray for healing for our loved ones, but we also often see times when people we love (or ourselves) are simply not healed.

Who Touched Me?

A woman, very much like Shari, heard about a great miracle worker who was coming to her town. This man drew large crowds, and some said He could heal any disease. This woman had pursued every single doctor and medical advancement of her time, but to no avail.

> As Jesus went, the people pressed around him. And there was a woman who had had a discharge of blood for twelve years, and though she had spent all her living on physicians, she could not be healed by anyone (Luke 8:42–43).

We can't begin to comprehend all of the ramifications of this woman's condition. Her physical ailment would have made her ceremonially unclean, and therefore it was a violation of the law for her to join in public worship, or even to have any physical contact with another person (Lev. 15:19–27). Can you imagine neither touching, nor being touched by, another human being for 12 years?! How she must have longed for not only healing, but for physical affection once again.

> She came up behind him and touched the fringe of his garment, and immediately her discharge of blood ceased. And Jesus said, "Who was it that touched me?" When all denied it, Peter said, "Master, the crowds surround you and are pressing in on you!" But Jesus said, "Someone touched me, for I perceive that power has gone out from me" (Luke 8:44–46).

It is interesting to note here that Jesus felt "power" or "virtue" go out from Him. The Greek indicates that the crowd was nearly crushing Jesus! Not everyone who touched Jesus received a healing that day. This was no accidental touch on the part of the woman. This was planned and premeditated.

> She had heard the reports about Jesus and came up behind him in the crowd and touched his garment. For she said, "If I touch even his garments, I will be made well." And immediately the flow of blood dried up, and she felt in her body that she was healed of her disease (Mark 5:27–29).

Jesus waited for the person who had received His healing power to come forward, of her own will. Can you imagine how intimidating it must have been for the woman to admit what she had done? Not only was it culturally unacceptable for a woman to touch a man who was not her husband, but she had just broken the law! Why did Jesus ask this question? Did He honestly have no idea who had been healed? Was He singling out the woman, seeking to publicly humiliate her?

One person in the midst of that throng of people knew that something miraculous had just happened. She was healed. Now everyone looked around, waiting, to see if the guilty party would come forward.

And when the woman saw that she was not hidden, she came trembling, and falling down before him declared in the presence of all the people why she had touched him, and how she had been immediately healed. And he said to her, "Daughter, your faith has made you well; go in peace" (Luke 8:47–48).

Her public confession of her healing paved the way for her to be integrated back into society. Jesus spoke kindly to her, calling her "Daughter." Ironically, unlike the man who was healed at the pool of Bethesda, Jesus didn't seek out this woman. She sought out Jesus. She had great faith in Jesus, and that faith brought her healing.

Story of Healing

Dr. R.A. Torrey (1856–1928) was a graduate of Yale Divinity School and pastor of what is now known as Moody Church in Chicago. He received an honorary doctorate from Wheaton College and served as dean of what is now Biola University. He told this account of an experience he had during his first pastorate:

> A young man in my congregation, a dentist, was taken very sick. His father was a member of our church. I went to the home to see and talk with the young man, but he was unconscious, in the last stages of typhoid fever. One of the leading physicians of the town sat by his bedside and told me that the crisis was past and had passed the wrong way, that there was no hope whatever of his recovery. As I sat there an impulse came to me to kneel down and pray to God that He would heal the young man. I did this, and as I prayed a great assurance came into my heart that God had heard my prayer. I arose and said to the doctor, who was a backslider, "He will get well." The doctor smiled and replied, "Well, Mr. Torrey, that is all very well from your standpoint, but he cannot get well. The crisis is past and has passed the wrong way, and he will die." I replied,

"Doctor, that is all right from your standpoint, but God has heard my prayer. The man will not die, he cannot die at this time. He will get well." I returned to my home. A short time afterward they came up to tell me the young man was dying, that he was doing certain things that only one dying would do. I replied to them, "He is not dying, he cannot die now. He will get well." And get well he did, and as far as I know is living still, though that was over forty years ago.[1]

As we read through church history, we find seasons when God has chosen to glorify His name by doing what we consider to be the impossible, thereby confounding the wisdom of the wise.

Thoughts on Healing

I won't endeavor to attempt a full-scale treatise on the theology of physical healing, but I will suggest a few thoughts. In Mark's gospel, you don't get very far until you see Jesus being pressed by the crowds for miraculous healings. Jesus did, indeed, heal many people in Mark 1:29–34. However, He didn't ultimately plan on having a primary healing ministry.

In Mark 1:38, Jesus told Peter that He was going to move from town to town preaching, for that, He said, was the reason why He was on earth. Jesus emphasized preaching, the saving of men's souls, over the healing of their physical bodies. In fact, the same Jesus who healed blind eyes and withered hands also commanded us pluck them out, or cut them off, if they got in the way of our obedience to the gospel.

Three times the Apostle Paul asked the Lord to take away an affliction from him, but the response was no. "But he said to me, 'My grace is sufficient for you, for my power is made perfect in weakness.' Therefore I will boast all the more gladly of my weaknesses, so that the power of Christ may rest upon me" (2 Cor. 12:9).

---

1. R.A. Torrey, *Divine Healing: Does God Perform Miracles Today?* (originally printed in 1924 by Fleming H. Revell Company).

The answer to the why is Who. Jesus does not promise to deliver us from every difficulty, but He promises to conform us more and more into His image (Rom. 8:29). Joni Eareckson Tada, who became a quadriplegic at age 17, said at the 2014 "True Woman" conference, "God permits what He hates to achieve what He loves."[2] She also said, "Nothing could be more heavenly than finding Jesus in the middle of your hell."[3]

First Peter 4:1 declares that whoever has suffered in his body is done with sin. It appears, from Scripture, that sometimes God allows physical suffering, which was not His original design or plan, in order to help us see our complete and total dependency on Him for all things. "Jesus answered, 'It was not that this man sinned, or his parents, but that the works of God might be displayed in him' " (John 9:3).

Romans 8:28 informs us that God causes all things to work together for good (not that everything is good in itself), for those who are the called according to His purpose. I believe that God can and does heal people today. But I also believe that He is more concerned with our souls than these temporary bodies that are going to die and pass away. We need to trust in the sovereignty of God, and if He decides that He wants to allow a physical malady to linger for a season, or until He calls us home, I trust that we will be like Job and sing out, "Though he slay me, I will hope in him" (Job 13:15).

---

2. Joni E. Tada and Steve Estes, *When God Weeps* (Grand Rapids, MI: Zondervan, 1997), p. 84.

3. http://www.truewoman.com/?id=2952.

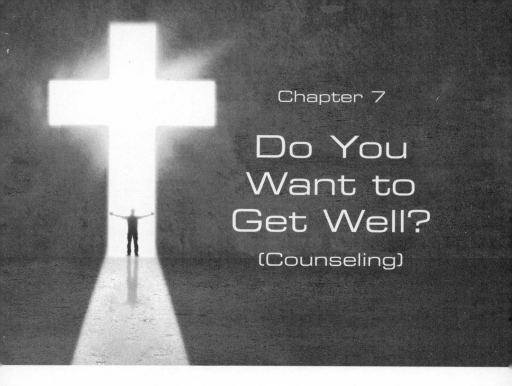

Chapter 7

Do You Want to Get Well?

(Counseling)

I 'll never forget the day I entered a recovery class for people who were trying to stop smoking. I felt so uncomfortable as I looked around the room, feeling as though I didn't really belong there. I have to admit, I could have never imagined a scenario compelling enough to get into a recovery group. It wasn't that I was too ashamed to admit that I had a problem, or that the addiction was too entrenched to let go; instead, the awkwardness came more from the fact that I had never smoked. I was accompanying a friend who was trying to quit.

I learned more that night about smoking than I ever wanted to. I learned every possible health and financial reason why I should quit. I was sold. But to be honest, smoking has always seemed about as desirable to me as sucking on my car's exhaust pipe, so it wasn't a hard sell.

For my friend, however, it was a deep struggle. Smoking was never something he took seriously until he went to the doctor. The doctor told him, "You have two choices. You can either stop smoking, or you can take at least ten years off your life expectancy." At that point, he had a serious choice in front of him. How important to him was his nearly 20-year cigarette addiction? Did he really want to stop? He wanted to quit, of course, but, then again, he didn't.

Do You Want to Get Well?

A friend of mine who is a Christian counselor once told me that one of the questions a counselor sometimes needs to ask a client is, "What do you hope to achieve from these counseling sessions?" If people don't have an end goal of being whole and moving forward in their lives, there is nothing the counselor can do to truly help them.

Jesus asked this question when He met blind Bartimaeus: "What do you want me to do for you?" Bartimaeus expressed his desire to have his sight return, and Jesus said, "Your faith has made you well." Jesus asked a similar question of a man who had a long history of physical disabilities.

While these stories are clearly referring to physical healing, I would like for us to consider how they apply to emotional healing as well.

Now there is in Jerusalem by the Sheep Gate a pool, in Aramaic called Bethesda, which has five roofed colonnades.[1] In these lay a multitude of invalids — blind, lame, and paralyzed. One man was there who had been an invalid for thirty-eight years[2] (John 5:2–5).

---

1. The unique five portico pool of Bethesda was discovered by archaeologists in the late 19th century. In 2005, the pool of Siloam (where Jesus healed a blind man, John 9) was discovered, and the two have been connected as twin pools. Both are believed to be *mikveh*, or special pools designed for ritual cleansing. In biblical times, it was located at the Sheep Gate. Today it is near St. Anne's Church in Jerusalem.

2. Mention of Jesus doing this miracle near the Sheep Gate may have served as a metaphor for the nation of Israel. Jesus, the Lamb of God, healed a man who was blind (see John 9:42), lame, and paralyzed for 38 years (perhaps harkening back to the nation of Israel wandering in the wilderness for 38 years — see Deut. 2:14). Spiritually, the nation of Israel needed the healing touch of Jesus as well.

When you have been doing something for 38 years, it's more than a habit; it's a deeply entrenched way of life. Every experience of this man's life for nearly four decades was inside the context of his disability. He knew nothing outside of his personal matrix.

> When Jesus saw him lying there and knew that he had already been there a long time, he said to him, "Do you want to be healed?" (John 5:6).

Doesn't this seem like a self-evident question? Why wouldn't the man want to get well? Would anyone in their right mind want to stay in that condition? Why did Jesus ask this question? What was it He wanted the man to consider about himself and his situation?

Being Stuck

In the original Greek language, it says that Jesus saw that man and "perceived," or "understood," that he had been there a long time. The *Pulpit Commentary* says of this verse:

> When Jesus saw him lying there, and perceived ([in the original Greek] came to know by his searching glance and intuitive knowledge of the history of others) that he had during a long time already been in that condition, or in sickness, said unto him — spontaneously, in the royalty of his benefactions, not demanding from the man even the faith to be healed, and dealing with him almost as he did with the dead — Wilt thou be made whole?[3]

It seems from the original Greek text that Jesus was not relying on a preconditioned knowledge, but rather the kind of intuition that comes from compassion. I believe that Jesus was setting an example for us in terms of how we do ministry to others. We need to be willing to look at their circumstances with a wide-angle lens, so to speak. You can almost never effectively minister to someone's needs unless you understand his or her broader context.

---

3. *Pulpit Commentary* (Peabody, MA: Hendrickson Publishers, 1990).

Jesus saw past the man's preconceived ideas of how he could be healed, and had compassion on him. Despite the immaturity of his theology (limiting God to a once-a-year event at the pool), the man wanted to get well, and Jesus responded to his desire.

There is nothing in this narrative to cause us to think that the man did anything special to attract Jesus' notice, and the man did not even know who Jesus was (vs. 13). The word *Bethesda* means "House of Mercy,"[4] and I believe that is just what this story emphasizes. It was all about Jesus and His great mercy, reaching out to a person with an obvious need.

God Does Things His Way and in His Timing

> The sick man answered him, "Sir, I have no one to put me into the pool when the water is stirred up, and while I am going, another steps down before me" (John 5:7).[5]

The man had a preconceived notion of how his personal healing was going to occur. This is a mistake we frequently make. We are often deceived into believing that God will do things the way we want, or expect, Him to. In this case, that man believed that his healing could come through getting into the pool when the angel stirred up the water.

His view was that he had to rely on the generosity, speed, and skill of another human to get him into the water. He believed the healing was always going to be for "the other guy" and not for him. Jesus was not bound by the man's concept of getting into the pool in order to get well.

---

4. Easton's Bible Dictionary, http://eastonsbibledictionary.org/.
5. If you look in most contemporary English Bibles, you will see that John 5:4 is omitted. Here it is in the KJV: "For an angel went down at a certain season into the pool, and troubled the water: whosoever then first after the troubling of the water stepped in was made whole of whatsoever disease he had." This verse is omitted, because many of the oldest manuscripts do not contain this verse. Some scholars believe it was a commentary footnote that was added into the text by later scribes; others believe it was in the original and taken out by early copyists. At any rate, this is the source of the tradition referred to by the paralyzed man.

Jesus said to him, "Get up, take up your bed, and walk." And at once the man was healed, and he took up his bed and walked (John 5:8–9).

You Can't Heal Yourself

If the man had the ability to simply "get up and walk," don't you think he would have done so before now? The man was told to do something that was not within his own power. The amazing thing was, he did it! Suppose, though, that he didn't believe. Suppose that he just continued to lie there, convinced that he would always be a cripple. He had to act, by faith, upon the command of Jesus.

You Can't Heal Others

We must always remember that only God can heal (physically or emotionally). God may use us as agents of grace in the life of another person, but the wisdom, power, and restoration belong to God alone.

We Help Others with the Help We Have Received from God

Charles Spurgeon (1834–1892) is known as the "Prince of Preachers." He is less known for having long bouts with serious depression. He told a story of being severely depressed one Sunday night. He felt truly forsaken by God because of circumstances in his life. However, he made himself preach a sermon, despite how he felt, and afterward a man came forward who Spurgeon described as being "as nearly insane as he could be to be out of an asylum." Spurgeon sought to comfort and counsel him and encouraged him to come back the next day, where he encouraged him further. Spurgeon heard no more from the man until five years later when Spurgeon was speaking on the text, "The Almighty hath vexed my soul."

After the service the man came forward and explained how Spurgeon's words had helped to lift him out of his pit. The man shared, "I am sure you will be glad to know that I have walked in the sunlight from that day till now. Everything is changed and altered with me."

Spurgeon realized that he was able to help that pitiful man most effectively because of the pain he felt in his own heart. He explained, "I blessed God that my fearful experience had prepared me to sympathize with him and guide him; but last night, when I saw him perfectly restored, my heart overflowed with gratitude to God for my former sorrowful feelings. I would go into the deeps a hundred times to cheer a downcast spirit: it is good for me to have been afflicted that I might know how to speak a word in season to one that is weary."[6]

> Blessed be the God and Father of our Lord Jesus Christ, the Father of mercies and God of all comfort, who comforts us in all our affliction, so that we may be able to comfort those who are in any affliction, with the comfort with which we ourselves are comforted by God (2 Cor. 1:3–4).

Wisdom from the Past

I often like to go back to writings from the past to see how people handled various issues in previous centuries. The great Puritan preacher Richard Baxter (1615–1691) wrote a small book to help believers overcome depression. He outlines the following ten points as guidelines or anchor points to help give stability to a Christian who is weathering storms of emotional pain and struggle:

1. Obey God in all things.
2. Hold fast to the sufficiency of the Bible as being God's Word, inspired by the Holy Spirit.
3. Allow others to help you understand and obey God's Word.
4. Do not view anything as necessary to Christianity or salvation that is not recorded in Scripture and has not

---

6. Charles Spurgeon, from his sermon "The Cost of Being a Soul-Winner," http://www.spurgeon.org/misc/sw09.htm.

been held necessary by all true Christians in every age and place.

5. Maintain the unity of the Spirit in the bond of peace with all true Christians, and live in communion with other believers.
6. Do not elevate any particular church group or sect above the universal Body of Christ.
7. Do not allow yourself to doubt what is clearly true.
8. Live up to all of the truth that you have learned so far.
9. Remember that everyone is imperfect and makes mistakes, and we all lack perfect knowledge.
10. Never stop learning and growing.[7]

It is interesting for me to think that almost four hundred years ago, Christians were struggling with the same difficulties we are, and godly men and women were seeking to provide biblical counsel to help guide them.

What Is Our Part

Dr. Jay Adams founded the practice of Nouthetic Counseling in 1969, based on the word that the Bible uses for "counsel": *nouthesia*.

> Now we ask you, brothers, to recognize those who labor among you, and manage you in the Lord, and *counsel* [*nouthesia*] you (1 Thess. 5:12).[8]

Confrontation, Concern, and Change

The three ideas found in the word *nouthesia* are confrontation, concern, and change. To put it simply, nouthetic counseling consists of lovingly confronting people out of deep concern in order to help them make those changes that God requires.[9]

7. Richard Baxter, *The Cure of Melancholy and Overmuch Sorrow, by Faith*, http://www.puritansermons.com/baxter/baxter25.htm.
8. This version of the Bible is from *The Christian Counselor's New Testament*, by Jay Adams (Grand Rapids, MI: Baker Book House, 1980).
9. http://www.nouthetic.org/about-ins/what-is-nouthetic-counseling.

Confrontation

Back to my story about my cigarette-addicted friend. Before he was willing to get help, he had to be confronted with the seriousness of his problem. Nowadays, confrontation is generally viewed as something to be avoided at all costs. While it is seldom pleasant, it is often necessary.

Some people are well aware of the seriousness of their condition and, therefore, don't need to be persuaded; others are in denial, and not yet ready to see themselves or their situation as it truly is.

Concern

The only things that I could do for my friend were to go along, encourage, pray, and provide accountability. Being a listening ear, asking questions, and encouraging people to pray and study the Holy Scriptures are all things we can and should do to help those for whom we care.

Change

We must realize, however, that we cannot provide the power, nor the desire for someone else to change. We only have sway over our own lives in this area. This is where the power of prayer is so important. We need to remember that, unless God intervenes on behalf of our loved ones, there is no hope. Nothing in this world has the ability to bring us back into proper alignment unless God supplies His blessing.

Whether the change is needed for us, or for our friends, the good news is that Jesus does not lack the power to heal and transform lives. There is no need for us to lie on a proverbial mat for 38 years, atrophying into spiritual and emotional paralysis. I believe Jesus is asking us, "Do you want to get well?"

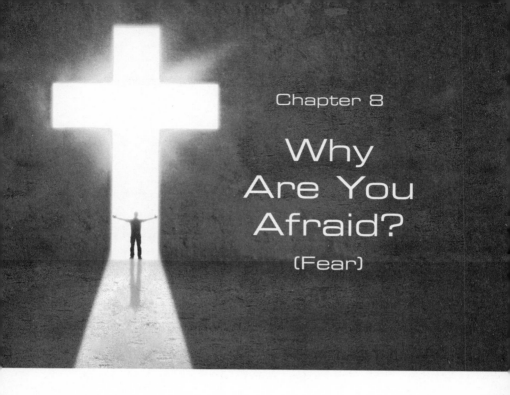

Chapter 8

Why Are You Afraid?

(Fear)

When I was a boy, I remember being afraid of the dark . . . until I learned that I wasn't. One day I heard a broadcast of Dr. James Dobson's radio show where he informed me (and his other listeners) that it wasn't actually "the dark" that frightened me. Instead, I was afraid of things that were IN the dark. That was a revelation. I'm not sure the distinction actually helped though.

Now I knew it was actually the bogeyman who lived in my closet, and under my bed, that scared the heebie-jeebies out of me, and not the darkness itself, but I was still afraid to sleep without the light on! In retrospect, when I consider the mess under my bed and in my closet, my fears were probably well founded!

All of us have phobias. In his first inaugural address, Franklin Delano Roosevelt declared, "The only thing we have to fear is fear itself." Personally, I find that anti-phobic thought to be tremendously comforting . . . until I consider all of the truly life-threatening dangers we all potentially face every day: terrorism, economic collapse, drunk drivers, thieves, super-viruses, earthquakes, tsunamis, fast food, and politicians.

Is it Okay to Fear?

Do you ever find yourself saying things like, "Well, I'm just worried that . . ." or "I'm afraid that . . ."?

Have you ever noticed in Scripture that just about any time God called someone to do a great and important task He prefaced the instruction with, "Fear not!"? Abraham (Genesis 15:1), Jacob (Genesis 46:3), Moses (Numbers 21:34), the children of Israel (Deuteronomy 1:21, 31:6), Joshua (Joshua 8:1), Daniel (Daniel 10:12), Joseph and Mary (Matthew 1:20; Luke 1:30), the shepherds abiding in the field (Luke 2:10), the Apostle Paul (Acts 27:24), and the Apostle John (Revelation 1:17) are just a few of the examples of those whom God instructed not to fear.

> "Have I not commanded you? Be strong and coura-geous. Do not be frightened, and do not be dismayed, for the LORD your God is with you wherever you go" (Josh. 1:9).

While it is common for us to fear, we need to ask ourselves, what part of "Fear not!" do we not understand?

When you tell your children not to do something and they bla-tantly disobey you, what do you do? I hope you correct them and teach them not to do that again. Well, as God's children, we have been specifically commanded not to be afraid. We are not allowed to worry, fret, be anxious, or dismayed.

> Do not be anxious about anything, but in everything by prayer and supplication with thanksgiving let your requests be made known to God. And the peace of God, which sur-passes all understanding, will guard your hearts and your minds in Christ Jesus" (Phil. 4:6–7).

When you find yourself being fearful about something, remember you are disregarding God's direct commands. Those panic-stricken moments are great opportunities to humble ourselves before our Maker and ask for His forgiveness. Just like Peter walking on the water, when we take our eyes off of Jesus, we start to sink.

To clarify, I'm not referring to the kind of fear we experience when we are being chased by an angry dog or falling off the roof. I'm speaking of the irrational fear we experience that is not from God, but from our adversary. We are told that a "spirit of fear" is not from God, but from the evil one (see Romans 8:15; 2 Timothy 1:7; 1 John 4:18).

Asleep in the Boat

Jesus' disciples found themselves in a situation where they thought their lives were about to be over.

> And when he got into the boat, his disciples followed him. And behold, there arose a great storm on the sea, so that the boat was being swamped by the waves; but he was asleep. And they went and woke him, saying, "Save us, Lord; we are perishing" (Matt. 8:23–25).

Were the disciples truly perishing? No, of course not. God had great plans for their lives that went far beyond that moment in the boat. They were in no more risk of dying at that moment than they were had they been sleeping soundly in their beds at home. They just didn't realize that truth. (In fact, Mark 4:38 informs us that Jesus was sound asleep in the boat. He wasn't worried a bit!)

> You keep him in perfect peace whose mind is stayed on you, because he trusts in you (Isa. 26:3).

Invincible until God Calls Us Home

Early in the morning of July 21, 1861, Thomas "Stonewall" Jackson sought the Lord in prayer before the first Battle of Manassas, asking for His divine will to be done. Later that day, the outnumbered Confederates took a beating. At one point, the southern army began to retreat because of the heat of the battle. Suddenly, General Bernard Bee shouted for the troops to look at General Jackson. He was sitting high in his saddle, with bullets and cannon fodder exploding around him. At one point, he was shot in his left hand. Bee's cry was heard over the noise of the battle, "Look men! There is Jackson, standing like a stone wall!"[1]

Jackson's courage inspired the men to regroup and fight bravely. By the end of the day, 111 Confederates had died, and 373 were missing. As Jackson knelt beside a dead soldier, Captain John D. Imboden asked him, "General, how is it you can keep so serene, and stay so utterly insensible, with a storm of shells and bullets about your head?"

Jackson replied, "Captain, my religious belief teaches me to feel as safe in battle as in bed. God has fixed the time for my death. I do not concern myself about that, but to be always ready, no matter when it may overtake me. Captain, that is the way all men should live, and then all would be equally brave."[2]

Why Are You Afraid?

Jesus' perspective is eternal; ours is often temporal. Jesus always sees and knows the big picture; we often get distracted by the wind, the waves, or the bullets swirling around us. Perspective is everything. Do we have a heavenly view, or a shortsighted, earthly one?

> And [Jesus] said to them, "Why are you afraid, O you of little faith?" Then he rose and rebuked the winds and the sea, and there was a great calm. And the men marveled, saying, "What sort of man is this, that even winds and sea obey him?" (Matt. 8:26–27).

Why do you think Jesus asked them why they were afraid? We know He saw the wind and waves that were troubling them. Do you think

---

1. This version of Bee's cry was published in the *Charleston Mercury* on July 25, 1861, and reprinted in the *Richmond Daily Dispatch* and *Lexington Gazette*.
2. Quoted in *Stonewall Jackson As Military Commander* by John Selby (New York: Barnes & Noble, Inc., 2000), p. 25.

Jesus was confused by the situation and their response, or do you think He was wanting them to ask this question to themselves? The disciples had in the boat with them the very same God who created the universe, the same God through whom we live and move and have our being (Acts 17:28), the same God who holds everything together by the strength of His power (Col. 1:17). The same scenario is true for us.

We Are in the Same Boat as the Disciples

God will never call us to do something and then neglect to equip us for the task.

There is only One whom we are commanded to fear, and we are sinning if we do not fear God. "And do not fear those who kill the body but cannot kill the soul. Rather fear him who can destroy both soul and body in hell" (Matt. 10:28).

It is impossible to truly fear God and your circumstance at the same time. We need to choose to "continue in the fear of the LORD all the day" (Prov. 23:17).

Fear is always caused by unbelief. We do not believe or trust God when we fear. Our belief in His sovereignty is shaken. We forget that nothing can happen to us that does not filter through His all-powerful, all-knowing, and all-loving hands. Worry is failing to believe that God will always act in the most loving and caring way on our behalf.

Another way of looking at this is that we will always be fearing something. We will either be fearing the Lord (having proper awe, reverence, and respect for who He is), or we will fear our situation, circumstance, and/or future. Just as we will always be worshiping something (either God, a false god, or ourselves), we cannot escape the mutually exclusive nature of the fear that is attached to worship. We will fear whatever we have put our trust in (money, security, etc.).

Charles Spurgeon (1834–1892) in his sermon, "Fear Not," said:

Make a man afraid — he will run at his own shadow; make a man brave, and he will stand before an army and overcome them. He will never do much good in the world who is afraid of men. The fear of God bringeth blessings, but the fear of men bringeth a snare, and such a snare that many feet have been tripped by it. No man shall be faithful to God, if he is fearful of man; no man shall find his arm sufficient for him, and his might equal to his emergencies unless he can confidently believe, and quietly wait. We must not fear; for fear is weakening.[3]

I am training my mind to look to the Lord every time I am afraid. I confess my sin of fear; I remember the One I am obligated to fear; I say, "The LORD is my light and my salvation; whom shall I fear? The LORD is the stronghold of my life; of whom shall I be afraid" (Ps. 27:1).

I don't care what the media tells me. It doesn't matter what my friends think or what society says I should believe. "When I am afraid, I put my trust in you. . . . In God I trust; I shall not be afraid. What can man do to me?" (Ps. 56:3, 11). I'm going to stop excusing fear as something I'm entitled to and turn it over to the Master. He is in the boat with me, and He will never let me drown.

---

3. http://www.spurgeon.org/sermons/0156.htm.

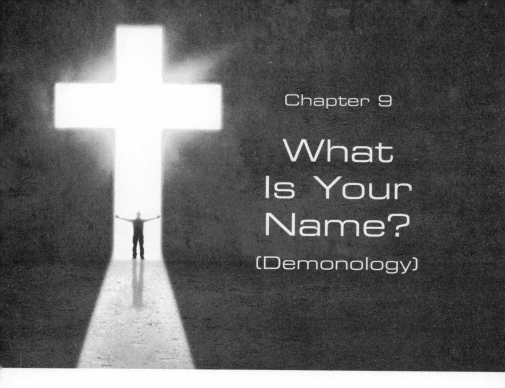

Chapter 9

What Is Your Name?

(Demonology)

When I was a teenager, a Christian novelist named Frank Peretti wrote a couple of fiction books about the demonic realm that made a really deep impact on Christendom. These books were a couple of the first runaway bestsellers in the Christian fiction genre. I often wonder what makes a book take off and become a phenomenon. Often, it is just in the right place at the right time, saying something of special relevance to people in that moment.

I think the topic of the spiritual realm (and the demonic in particular) exploded in the 1980s for a couple of reasons. First of all, very few people were hearing anything about demons from the pulpit, especially not on Mother's Day. I guess it's not considered a very warm and inviting topic. Second, Evangelicals had finally received information on the topic in a format that was palatable to them: a novel. If I had a dollar for every person who told me that *The Shack* changed the way they understood God, or that *The Da*

Vinci Code helped them to understand the historical Jesus, I'd be a wealthy man. But I digress.

The downside of this is that many people assumed that everything in the book was equal to the Word of God (certainly not the intent of the author!) and as a result, began almost literally looking for demons behind every bush.

The upside is that it renewed an important awareness of the spiritual realm and opened an entirely new conversation within the Church, which had been ignored and overlooked previously. I believe it is important for us to be biblically informed on this rather esoteric aspect of theology in order to avoid the myths and superstition that often surround it.

Jesus' Encounter with Demons

Jesus encountered demons on numerous occasions during His earthly ministry. Here is the story of one of those meetings:

> Then they sailed to the country of the Gerasenes, which is opposite Galilee. When Jesus had stepped out on land, there met him a man from the city who had demons. For a long time he had worn no clothes, and he had not lived in a house but among the tombs. When he saw Jesus, he cried out and fell down before him and said with a loud voice, "What have you to do with me, Jesus, Son of the Most High God? I beg you, do not torment me." For he had commanded the unclean spirit to come out of the man. (For many a time it had seized him. He was kept under guard and bound with chains and shackles, but he would break the bonds and be driven by the demon into the desert) (Luke 8:26–29).

It is important to note here the sheer terror exhibited by the demons in stark contrast to the composed nature of Jesus during this encounter. Jesus, who often didn't answer the questions of His critics, but instead responded with a question of His own, does so in this instance as well. He will not allow the demon to engage Him on the demon's terms.

> Jesus then asked him, "What is your name?" And he said, "Legion," for many demons had entered him. And they begged him not to command them to depart into the abyss. Now a large herd of pigs was feeding there on the hillside, and they begged him to let them enter these. So he gave them permission (Luke 8:30–32).

Why did Jesus ask this question? A name signifies authority and control. The answer reveals who was still in control of this man's life.

> Then the demons came out of the man and entered the pigs, and the herd rushed down the steep bank into the lake and drowned. When the herdsmen saw what had happened, they fled and told it in the city and in the country. Then people went out to see what had happened, and they came to Jesus and found the man from whom the demons had gone, sitting at the feet of Jesus, clothed and in his right mind, and they were afraid. And those who had seen it told them how the demon-possessed man had been healed. Then all the people of the surrounding country of the Gerasenes asked him to depart from them, for they were seized with great fear. So he got into the boat and returned. The man from whom the demons had gone begged that he might be with him, but Jesus sent him away, saying, "Return to your home, and declare how much God has done for you." And he went away, proclaiming throughout the whole city how much Jesus had done for him (Luke 8:33–39, see also Mark 5).

It is not abundantly clear to me whether Jesus directed his question to the demon, or to the man, but the demon(s) answered.

Matthew 8:24–28 says there were two demon-possessed men who were delivered, while Mark and Luke only mention one. Some skeptics point to this discrepancy as a supposed example of a contradiction in the Bible. The simple solution? There were two men, but Matthew decided to focus on both characters, while the other narratives honed in on only one. No contradiction.

Ten Things We Know about Demons

The Bible doesn't tell us a whole lot about demons; however, we do get some fascinating insights into these fiendish beings.

1. They were created by Jesus and are not eternally existent.

All things were made through [Jesus], and without him was not any thing made that was made (John 1:3).

For by [Jesus] all things were created, in heaven and on earth, visible and invisible, whether thrones or dominions or rulers or authorities — all things were created through him and for him (Col. 1:16).

2. They were created good, but chose to rebel against God and were cast down to earth.

And God saw everything that he had made, and behold, it was very good (Gen. 1:31).

Many theologians believe that Isaiah 14:12–15 and Exodus 28:14–19 are symbolically describing the revolt and overthrow of Lucifer (referred to metaphorically as the Prince of Tyre), the chief of the angels, who rebelled against God and brought a third of all of the created angels into revolt with him (see Rev. 12:4).

Now war arose in heaven, Michael and his angels fighting against the dragon. And the dragon and his angels fought back, but he was defeated, and there was no longer any place for them in heaven. And the great dragon was thrown down, that ancient serpent, who is called the devil and Satan, the deceiver of the whole world — he was thrown down to the earth, and his angels were thrown down with him (Rev. 12:7–9).

Therefore, rejoice, O heavens and you who dwell in them! But woe to you, O earth and sea, for the devil has come down to you in great wrath, because he knows that his time is short! (Rev. 12:12).

3. Demons can and do make residence inside of human beings.

When the unclean spirit has gone out of a person, it passes through waterless places seeking rest, but finds none. Then it says, "I will return to my house from which I came." And when it comes, it finds the house empty, swept, and put in order. Then it goes and brings with it seven other spirits more evil than itself, and they enter and dwell there, and the last state of that person is worse than the first. So also will it be with this evil generation (Matt. 12:43–45).

4. Demons have power, but they are not omniscient, omnipresent, or eternally existent.

Demons have strong powers, but they do not possess the incommunicable attributes of God (see "The Communicato Idiomatum" in the appendix). There is no biblical indication they can read people's minds, know the future (beyond what has been prophesied), or inhabit Christians (see Matt. 6:24, Rom. 8:9–10, 1 Cor. 12:3).

5. Demons seem to be territorial and jurisdictional.

In the Scripture, demons are often referred to as princes. They seem to have geographical jurisdiction in some way. In Daniel 10:12–13, the angel talks about attempting to answer Daniel's request for help, but being held up by the "Prince of Persia." In verse 20 he explains that he is heading to fight against the "Prince of Persia" and the "Prince of Greece," with the heavenly angel, Michael, who is also called a "prince."

Jesus spoke of the city of Pergamum as being the physical ruling place for Satan, the fallen angel. "I know where you dwell, where Satan's throne is" (Rev. 2:13). A throne speaks of authority within a sphere or realm. Ephesians 6:12 speaks of the warfare in which we are engaged with these demons: "For we do not wrestle against flesh and blood, but against the rulers, against the authorities, against the cosmic powers over this present darkness, against the spiritual forces of evil in the heavenly places."

Even though they have power, they are still ultimately subject to the authority of God (see Job 1:6, 2:1, Matt. 4:10, Luke 22:31–21).

6. Jesus has all power and authority over demons.

> And Jesus came and said to them, "All authority in heaven and on earth has been given to me" (Matt. 28:18).

> Therefore God has highly exalted him and bestowed on him the name that is above every name, so that at the name of Jesus every knee should bow, in heaven and on earth and under the earth, and every tongue confess that Jesus Christ is Lord, to the glory of God the Father (Phil. 2:9–11).

> "What have you to do with us, Jesus of Nazareth? Have you come to destroy us? I know who you are — the Holy One of God!" (Mark 1:24).

There was an accusation leveled at Jesus that He was so successful against the "dark side," because He was of the dark side Himself. Jesus explained that a kingdom can't undermine itself and be successful.

> But some of them said, "He casts out demons by Beelzebul, the prince of demons," while others, to test him, kept seeking from him a sign from heaven. But he, knowing their thoughts, said to them, "Every kingdom divided against itself is laid waste, and a divided household falls. And if Satan also is divided against himself, how will his

kingdom stand? For you say that I cast out demons by Beelzebul. And if I cast out demons by Beelzebul, by whom do your sons cast them out? Therefore they will be your judges. But if it is by the finger of God that I cast out demons, then the kingdom of God has come upon you" (Luke 11:15–20).

7. It is the authority of Jesus alone that drives out demons.

Neither Jesus, nor the Apostles, ever engaged in the hokey rituals of modern-day televangelists or exorcists when it came to dealing with demons. They never laid hands on possessed people, anointed them with oil or holy water, or performed extensive rituals. Jesus and the Apostles spoke to the demons, commanding them to come out of the person they possessed — and they did.

There is no mere incantation or mantra that will suffice. When a group of individuals tried to invoke the name of Jesus, apart from relationship with, and empowerment by, Him, things went really bad.

> Then some of the itinerant Jewish exorcists undertook to invoke the name of the Lord Jesus over those who had evil spirits, saying, "I adjure you by the Jesus whom Paul proclaims." Seven sons of a Jewish high priest named Sceva were doing this. But the evil spirit answered them, "Jesus I know, and Paul I recognize, but who are you?" And the man in whom was the evil spirit leaped on them, mastered all of them and overpowered them, so that they fled out of that house naked and wounded (Acts 19:13–16).

Only the power of Jesus is able to cast out evil spirits. Jesus asked, "And if Satan casts out Satan, he is divided against himself. How then will his kingdom stand?" (Matt. 12:26).

Corrie Ten Boom (1892–1983), wrote: "We have a good safeguard and guide, the Bible, God's Word. Here we find not only the necessary information about Satan and demons, but also the weapons and the armor that we need for this battle, so that, through Jesus Christ, we may be more than conquerors."[1]

8. Faith, and often fasting and prayer, is essential in driving out a demon.

> And someone from the crowd answered him, "Teacher, I brought my son to you, for he has a spirit that makes him mute. And whenever it seizes him, it throws him down, and he foams and grinds his teeth and becomes rigid. So I asked your disciples to cast it out, and they were not able." And he answered them, "O faithless generation, how long am I to be with you? How long am I to bear with you? Bring him to me" (Mark 9:17–19).

Here are two other seemingly rhetorical questions Jesus asked. He is obviously disappointed at their unbelief.

> And they brought the boy to him. And when the spirit saw him, immediately it convulsed the boy, and he fell on the ground and rolled about, foaming at the mouth. And Jesus asked his father, "How long has this been happening to him?" And he said, "From childhood. And it has often cast him into fire and into water, to destroy him. But if you can do anything, have compassion on us and help us." And Jesus said to him, " 'If you can!' All things are possible for one who believes." Immediately the father of the child cried out and said, "I believe; help my unbelief!" And when Jesus saw that a crowd came running together, he rebuked the unclean spirit, saying to it, "You mute and deaf spirit, I command you, come out of him and never enter him again." And after crying out and convulsing him terribly, it came out, and the boy was like a corpse, so that most of

---

1. Corrie Ten Boom, *Defeated Enemies* (Fort Washington, PA: CLC Publications, 2008), p. 7.

them said, "He is dead." But Jesus took him by the hand and lifted him up, and he arose (Mark 9:20–27).

Then the disciples came to Jesus privately and said, "Why could we not cast it out?" He said to them, "Because of your little faith. For truly, I say to you, if you have faith like a grain of mustard seed, you will say to this mountain, 'Move from here to there,' and it will move, and nothing will be impossible for you" (Matt. 17:19–21).

9. Hell wasn't originally created for humans but for the devil and his angels.

Then he will say to those on his left, "Depart from me, you cursed, into the eternal fire prepared for the devil and his angels" (Matt. 25:41).

The place of eternal fire, commonly called hell, was created for the purpose of eternal punishment for these rebellious beings.

10. Final and certain eternal judgment awaits Satan and his angels.

"They begged him not to command them to depart into the abyss" (Luke 8:31).

And the devil who had deceived them was thrown into the lake of fire and sulfur where the beast and the false prophet were, and they will be tormented day and night forever and ever (Rev. 20:10).

How Many Demons Are There?

Most historians say that a Roman legion consisted of about 3,000 to 6,000 soldiers.

Jesus said, "Do you think that I cannot appeal to my Father, and he will at once send me more than twelve legions of angels?" (Matt. 26:53).

If we were to take the larger number (the amount of a full legion) of 6,000 as our guide, we could conclude that there are at least 72,000 angels in the universe. According to the interpretation of most biblical scholars, one-third of the originally created angels revolted against God, which would mean that there were at least 108,000 originally created angels, 36,000 of whom became demons when they were cast to the earth. That means that, with a 7 billion person population on the earth, there is, at least, about one demon for every 20,000 people. There could, of course, be far more than that. So, the next time you visit New York City, keep in mind that there are at least 432 demons running around there! It is even rumored that some of them might be driving some of those taxicabs! (Just kidding!)

My point here is not, of course, to provide an accurate census of the demonic population. It is rather to illustrate that, while we don't often give it significant thought, there is an unseen realm that is always active, operating all around us to accomplish their otherworldly agenda.

What Can We Learn from This Study of Demons?

James 2:19 says, "You believe that there is one God. Good! Even the demons believe that — and shudder" (NIV).

Simply believing in the existence, or even the power of God, isn't sufficient to save us. Having a fear of God is not enough to save us. Believing that Jesus is God will not save us (see Mark 1:24). Knowing the Bible (better than most Christians), and understanding biblical prophecy won't save us. The demons do all these things.

What is required for salvation is what the Bible refers to as "faith." Faith is believing God (not doubting or accusing Him) and putting our trust in Him. We believe, by faith, that Jesus has satisfied our incalculable debt to God and stands before God on our behalf, as our Savior and Lord. It is the indwelling of the Holy Spirit inside us that protects and seals us against the power of the enemy.

The Spirit within us also helps us to discern the Spirit of God from an unclean spirit.

> Beloved, do not believe every spirit, but test the spirits to see whether they are from God, for many false prophets have gone out into the world. By this you know the Spirit of God: every spirit that confesses that Jesus Christ has come in the flesh is from God, and every spirit that does not confess Jesus is not from God. This is the spirit of the antichrist, which you heard was coming and now is in the world already. Little children, you are from God and have overcome them, for he who is in you is greater than he who is in the world (1 John 4:1–4).

Jesus is supreme over the realms of darkness, and through His Resurrection from the dead, He made a way for us to live eternally with Him. By faith, we have nothing to fear, in this life, or in the life to come.

> For I am sure that neither death nor life, nor angels nor rulers, nor things present nor things to come, nor powers, nor height nor depth, nor anything else in all creation, will be able to separate us from the love of God in Christ Jesus our Lord (Rom. 8:38–39).

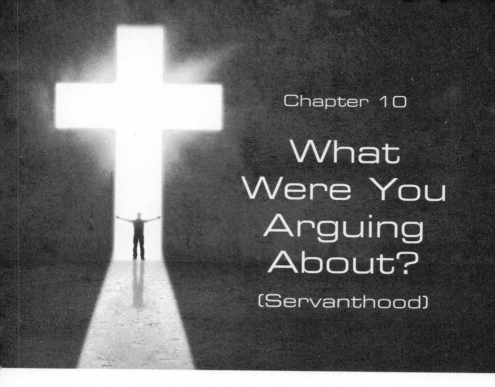

Chapter 10

What Were You Arguing About?

(Servanthood)

I t's amazing how we can often do the right things for the wrong reasons. Like studying the Bible to become popular and attract girls. Not something you've ever done? Well, I have. A long time ago. Let me explain. When I was about 14 years old, our church had a Bible quiz competition for the youth. Nearly all of the churches in our denomination participated in monthly district meets. Whoever won the district events would move on to the national competition.

Our church was small and had never won the district event. Since I was now a freshman, I was eligible to be on the high school team. I was generally interested and looking forward to participating, until I heard about "him." There was apparently a senior named Rich who had been the top quizzer in the district for three years in a row. All of the youth from our church were intimidated by his amazing Bible-quizzing prowess.

"We don't even bother to stand up for any of the questions until Rich quizzes out (answering five questions correctly). It's not worth trying. He's too fast, too smart, too amazing."

I had never met Rich, but his reputation indeed seemed daunting. When the first district event arrived, I discovered that his legend wasn't limited to the young people in our church. Everyone was "oohing" and "ahhing" about how great Rich was, and no one could possibly beat him. Everyone. Especially the cool girls. The whole event was all about Rich this, and Rich that. I quickly grew sick of it.

What made things worse was that Rich was not only a senior, but he was also innately cool, inordinately polite, and good looking. He quizzed out with no errors that first day. But then, so did I.

On the drive back home in the church bus, I continued to hear my peers (especially the cool girls) rant and rave about "Rich the Great." It was then and there that I made up my mind. This was war!

It didn't matter that I wasn't cool, well cultured, or handsome. It didn't matter that I was a gangly freshman with acne and awkward social skills. I was going to win this competition if it killed me! The great and stupendous Rich was going down in flames! I was going to kick his proverbial tail (in Christian love, of course!).

We were studying the Book of Matthew that year. I set out to practically memorize that entire book. I read the chapters forward and backward. There was a fire in my eye. Rich's rule as the "King of Quizzing" was about to end! Each month was nip and tuck. I would quiz out with no errors, but so did Rich. We were neck and neck. All of the other quizzers kept telling me to hang it up. They claimed I could never beat Rich. He was just too good.

It all came down to the last event. Rich arrived just before it started because he had to take a SAT test that morning. Once again, the weight of power went back and forth as we each vied for the lead position. Finally, on a question where Rich beat me to the buzzer, he just froze. His mind went blank, and for the life of him, he couldn't think of the answer. As amazing as it seemed, the mighty Rich was human after all. I don't know which event surprised me more — the fact that Rich hadn't won, or the fact that I did. As a tribute to sheer determination and effort, I quizzed out the entire season with no errors.

When the award ceremony arrived, I eagerly anticipated receiving the coveted trophy. Rich received his second-place award to the sound of thunderous ovation from our peers. My first-place title was met with a polite round of applause, and lots of comments later about how Rich would have won the title for the fourth year in a row, if only he hadn't had a test that distracted him that morning.

In that moment, the harsh realization came crashing down upon me. Rich wasn't popular and cool because he had won a small, district Bible-quizzing competition. Rich was popular and cool because he was . . . well . . . popular and cool. The thing I was really hoping for in winning was not to gain a greater understanding of the Scriptures, but rather to be liked by people who didn't respect me. I was engaged in trying to do the right things for all the wrong reasons.

What Were You Arguing About?

Jesus' disciples, I believe, had a similar experience. They were pursuing a good thing (the Kingdom of God) for many of the wrong reasons. Signing up to be Jesus' followers I'm sure made them feel they were part of the next big thing. They believed Christ's Kingdom was about to emerge in power and liberation, to bring a restoration to the nation of Israel. They were the key players in this new and exciting revolution that was about to take place.

However, Jesus' view of the Kingdom was quite different from the disciples'. The plan of the Father included suffering and dying, not immediate ruling and reigning. Jesus was about to confront the preconceived ideas and perceptions of His 12 followers.

> They came to Capernaum. When he was in the house, he asked them, "What were you arguing about on the road?" But they kept quiet because on the way they had argued about who was the greatest (Mark 9:33–34; NIV).

Why did Jesus ask this question? In Luke 9:47, we are told that Jesus knew their thoughts. So this question was definitely not for His benefit, to enlighten Him about the conversation, but rather to give the disciples an opportunity to be honest about the condition of their hearts.

Ironically, both Mark and Luke's gospels place the sequence of this event immediately after recording the failure of the disciples to assist a demon-possessed boy. Jesus had just rebuked them for their lack of faith. It seems extremely out of place for them to now be boasting about which of them was more important. But such is the human ego. It is so often blinded to reality by the fantasy or illusion we choose to imagine about ourselves.

So Jesus decided to use a visual illustration of what the Kingdom truly looks like.

> And he sat down and called the twelve. And he said to them, "If anyone would be first, he must be last of all and servant of all." And he took a child and put him in the midst of them, and taking him in his arms, he said to them, "Whoever receives one such child in my name receives me, and whoever receives me, receives not me but him who sent me" (Mark 9:35–37).

In Jesus' day, children were not often esteemed by the culture. They were there to serve, not to be served (in the Aramaic language, the words *servant* and *child* were the same). Jesus turned the prevailing paradigm on its head. The gospel gives importance and prominence to the lowest and the least.

Servanthood

Jesus reiterated this lesson again in the final meal He shared together with His disciples. He took the basin and the towel and proceeded to engage in the very lowest and most menial task of His day: washing the feet of His students. He then asked them another question:

"Do you understand what I have done to you?" (John 13:12).

Peter's request for Jesus to wash his head and hands as well probably indicates that the disciples were trying to embrace the new liturgy, without really understanding the principle behind it.

"You call me Teacher and Lord, and you are right, for so I am. If I then, your Lord and Teacher, have washed your feet, you also ought to wash one another's feet. For I have given you an example, that you also should do just as I have done to you. Truly, truly, I say to you, a servant is not greater than his master, nor is a messenger greater than the one who sent him. If you know these things, blessed are you if you do them" (John 13:13–17).

The world measures success by how many people you have working for, and serving, you. Jesus' standard of greatness is determined by how many people you are selflessly serving.

Can You Drink from This Cup?

Then the mother of the sons of Zebedee came up to him with her sons, and kneeling before him she asked him for something. And he said to her, "What do you want?" (Matt. 20:20–21).

Jesus gave the wife of Zebedee the chance to reveal her priorities. If Jesus was a genie in a bottle, and could grant one wish to this mother, what would she choose? In typical fashion, she revealed the heart of a mother. She asked nothing for herself, but instead she requested the greatest thing she could imagine on behalf of her two sons.

She said to him, "Say that these two sons of mine are to sit, one at your right hand and one at your left, in your kingdom." Jesus answered, "You do not know what you are asking. Are you able to drink the cup that I am to drink?" They said to him, "We are able" (Matt. 20:21–22).

Jesus turned the question to the disciples. Did they truly want what this entailed? Did they realize that glory is found through the path of suffering and abasement?

> He said to them, "You will drink my cup, but to sit at my right hand and at my left is not mine to grant, but it is for those for whom it has been prepared by my Father." And when the ten heard it, they were indignant at the two brothers. But Jesus called them to him and said, "You know that the rulers of the Gentiles lord it over them, and their great ones exercise authority over them. It shall not be so among you. But whoever would be great among you must be your servant, and whoever would be first among you must be your slave, even as the Son of Man came not to be served but to serve, and to give his life as a ransom for many" (Matt. 20:23–28).

Humility

In his book *Humility*, published in 1895, Andrew Murray (1828–1917), a missionary to South Africa, wrote:

> To know the humble man, to know how the humble man behaves, you must follow him in the common course of daily life. Is not this what Jesus taught? It was when the disciples disputed who should be greatest; when He saw how the Pharisees loved the chief place at feasts and the chief seats in the synagogues; when He had given them the example of washing their feet, that He taught His lessons of humility. Humility before God is nothing if not proved in humility before men.[1]

---

1. Andrew Murray, *Humility*, chapter 6, http://www.worldinvisible.com/library/ murray/5f00.0565/5f00.0565.06.htm

Jesus did not teach in the abstract. He led by example. We are told that we should emulate His posture of humble submission to the will of the Father.

> Do nothing from selfish ambition or conceit, but in humility count others more significant than yourselves. Let each of you look not only to his own interests, but also to the interests of others. Have this mind among yourselves, which is yours in Christ Jesus, who, though he was in the form of God, did not count equality with God a thing to be grasped, but emptied himself, by taking the form of a servant, being born in the likeness of men. And being found in human form, he humbled himself by becoming obedient to the point of death, even death on a cross (Phil. 2:3–8).

What is it about the human psyche that seems to crave adulation and admiration? Why do we try to orchestrate the universe so we always come out ahead, even at the expense of those we claim to love? Why is it so hard to be overlooked, or to fail to receive the credit for our accomplishments? It is this self-exalting egotism that eats away at the core of our being. It was infused into our DNA the moment we are conceived, and it gnaws away at our souls, desperately clutching at us. Pride seeks to separate us from the very purpose for which we were made: the worship of our Creator.

The Bible teaches us that Jesus, through His death on the Cross, put an end to the grip of sin upon our lives. Through the Holy Spirit (the gift He sent to empower us), we can put to death the power of pride over our lives.

Humble Yourself

> Humble yourselves before the Lord, and he will exalt you (James 4:10).

God will not allow pride to stand in His presence. You and I basically have two choices:

1. We can humble ourselves.
2. God will humble us.

You save a humble people, but your eyes are on the haughty to bring them down (2 Sam. 22:28).

When pride comes, then comes disgrace, but with humility comes wisdom (Prov. 11:2; NIV).

Pride goes before destruction, and a haughty spirit before a fall (Prov. 16:18).

Before destruction a man's heart is haughty, but humility comes before honor (Prov. 18:12).

One's pride will bring him low, but he who is lowly in spirit will obtain honor (Prov. 29:23).

For the LORD of hosts has a day against all that is proud and lofty, against all that is lifted up — and it shall be brought low (Isa. 2:12).

I tell you that this man, rather than the other, went home justified before God. For all those who exalt themselves will be humbled, and those who humble themselves will be exalted (Luke 18:14; NIV).

But he gives us more grace. That is why Scripture says: "God opposes the proud but shows favor to the humble" (James 4:6; NIV).

The Goal is NOT Low Self-Esteem, It's Less Self-Esteem

In a chapter entitled "The Great Sin," C.S. Lewis explains how humility is not about thinking less of ourselves, but rather, it is about thinking of ourselves less.

The real rest of being in the presence of God is, that you either forget about yourself altogether or see yourself as a small, dirty object. It is better to forget about yourself altogether.[2]

The purpose of humility is not asceticism, where we slip into a kind of sequestered monastic existence, hidden away from the world. The biblical mandate is to roll up our sleeves and serve others, for their sake, and the glory of God, rather than for our own praise.

Jesus said, "Beware of practicing your righteousness before other people in order to be seen by them, for then you will have no reward from your Father who is in heaven" (Matt. 6:1).

The enemy of our souls will use a good thing (service for God), and tempt us to apply the wrong motive (self-promotion), to lead us down a destructive path. It is only by relying on the example of Jesus, and the power of the Holy Spirit, that we can learn to love and serve others the way Jesus did.

> But this is the one to whom I will look: he who is humble and contrite in spirit and trembles at my word (Isa. 66:2).

---

2. C.S. Lewis, *Mere Christianity* (New York, NY: Harper Collins, 1952, 2001), p. 25.

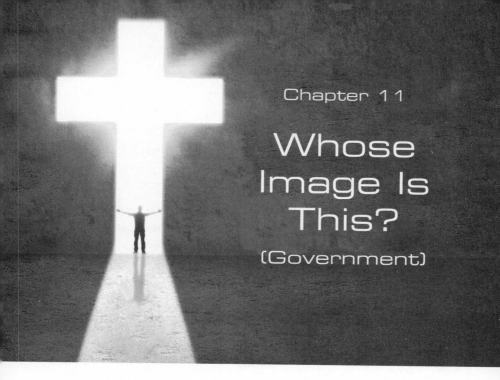

Chapter 11

Whose Image Is This?

(Government)

A number of years ago I got my first passport. It is still valid, and I use it when I travel. It gets me anywhere in the world I want to be because it is an internationally recognized government photo ID. That's the good news. The bad news is, the picture on it doesn't help the airport security much. You see, it was taken back when I still had hair! They always spend several awkward seconds comparing the younger, better-looking version I used to be, and the heavier, balding version I've become! Thankfully, it hasn't been rejected yet.

Photo ID is relatively new, but for thousands of years, people have used stamped images for identification. The oldest known stamped coins date back to about 700–600 B.C. and have been found in places like India, China, and Greece. A name and an image speak not only of identity, but also of authority. We have authority over what belongs to us.

When it comes to people, there has always been a tension throughout time regarding ownership and authority. Many human rulers have enslaved people and viewed the people under their rule as property, who exist to do their bidding. Tyrants view people as a commodity and declare ownership of the people's time and the fruit of their labors. Some dictators have chosen to take only a portion of the people's earnings, through taxation, and have "benevolently" allowed some of their servants to retain a percentage for their own personal use.

This tension between the ownership of humans and their labor was very much still in debate in Judea when Jesus began His ministry. Jesus was teaching that humans belonged to God and owed Him their devotion and service. The Roman Empire made an equal claim. This conflict met in a question that Jesus was asked, in an attempt to trap Him, and create a conflict between the Kingdom He was promoting, and the dominant one that ruled the Israelites with an iron fist.

God Is the Supreme Ruler of the Earth

So who is really in charge of things? Human governments or God? Let's see what the Scripture says on this issue.

Genesis 18:25 calls God "the judge of all the earth."

Then the LORD raised up judges (Judg. 2:16).

For the LORD is our judge; the LORD is our lawgiver; the LORD is our king; he will save us (Isa. 33:22).[1]

I saw in the night visions, and behold, with the clouds of heaven there came one like a son of man, and he came to the Ancient of Days and was presented before him. And to him was given dominion and glory and a kingdom, that all peoples, nations, and languages should serve him; his

---

1. As a side note, it is interesting to observe that this verse shows a distinction between the three branches of our American constitutional republic: the Judicial, the Legislative, and the Executive branches. Many of our Founding Fathers recognized, from this verse, that God was the ultimate authority over every branch of human government.

dominion is an everlasting dominion, which shall not pass away, and his kingdom one that shall not be destroyed (Dan. 7:13–14).

This passage in Daniel is a Messianic prophecy referring to Jesus, and the power that would belong to Him over the nations of this world. This promise is reiterated in the New Testament as well.

For in him the whole fullness of deity dwells bodily, and you have been filled in him, who is the head of all rule and authority (Col. 2:9–10).

And being found in human form, he humbled himself by becoming obedient to the point of death, even death on a cross. Therefore God has highly exalted him and bestowed on him the name that is above every name, so that at the name of Jesus every knee should bow, in heaven and on earth and under the earth, and every tongue confess that Jesus Christ is Lord, to the glory of God the Father (Phil. 2:8–11).

There is only one lawgiver and judge, he who is able to save and to destroy (James 4:12).

Some people claim that Jesus wasn't interested in earthly kingdoms, but only in the heavenly Kingdom. I don't believe this is true. He had to be concerned about earthly kingdoms, because the Bible teaches they were created by God. He did, however, recognize the difference between the two, and the fact that the earthly kingdoms serve a very limited purpose, for a designated time.

There are two popular (opposite) views regarding government gaining momentum in our culture:

1. The government is responsible to feed us, house us, educate us, and provide for our health care and retirement (socialism).
2. Government is bad and should be extremely limited or abolished altogether (libertarianism and anarchy).

Government Is Established by God

The biblical view is neither of these. The Bible teaches that all government is created by God. Everything God creates is "very good." However, like the rest of creation, corruption has entered the world through man's sin, and human government often reflects that brokenness and fallenness.

> Be subject for the Lord's sake to every human institution, whether it be to the emperor as supreme, or to governors as sent by him to punish those who do evil and to praise those who do good. For this is the will of God, that by doing good you should put to silence the ignorance of foolish people. Live as people who are free, not using your freedom as a cover-up for evil, but living as servants of God. Honor everyone. Love the brotherhood. Fear God. Honor the emperor (1 Pet. 2:13–17).

This epistle was written during the reign of the Roman emperors, so there is no chance that Peter thought the ruler himself was good. There was widespread persecution of Christians under Vespasian and Nero during the first century. Yet, in spite of that, the Apostles did not advocate for abolition of civil government, but rather submission to it. Paul reinforced this view.

The Biblical Role of Government

> Let every person be subject to the governing authorities. For there is no authority except from God, and those that exist have been instituted by God. Therefore whoever resists the authorities resists what God has appointed, and those who resist will incur judgment. For rulers are not a terror to good conduct, but to bad. Would you have no fear of the one who is in authority? Then do what is good, and you will receive his approval, for he is God's servant for your good. But if you do wrong, be afraid, for he does not bear the sword in vain. For

he is the servant of God, an avenger who carries out God's wrath on the wrongdoer. Therefore one must be in subjection, not only to avoid God's wrath but also for the sake of conscience. For because of this you also pay taxes, for the authorities are ministers of God, attending to this very thing. Pay to all what is owed to them: taxes to whom taxes are owed, revenue to whom revenue is owed, respect to whom respect is owed, honor to whom honor is owed (Rom. 13:1–7).

The biblical view of civil government is that it is not bad, but is to be extremely limited: to protect the citizens who do good, and punish those who do wrong.

Civil Disobedience

While the Bible teaches obedience and submission to governing authorities, it also teaches the necessity for nonviolent civil disobedience in any case where you are mandated to sin.

> So they called them and charged them not to speak or teach at all in the name of Jesus. But Peter and John answered them, "Whether it is right in the sight of God to listen to you rather than to God, you must judge, for we cannot but speak of what we have seen and heard" (Acts 4:18–20).

> And when they had brought them, they set them before the council. And the high priest questioned them, saying, "We strictly charged you not to teach in this name, yet here you have filled Jerusalem with your teaching, and you intend to bring this man's blood upon us." But Peter and the apostles answered, "We must obey God rather than men" (Acts 5:27–29).

Ultimate Allegiance

> Then the Pharisees went and plotted how to entangle him in his words. And they sent their disciples to him, along

> with the Herodians, saying, "Teacher, we know that you are
> true and teach the way of God truthfully, and you do not care
> about anyone's opinion, for you are not swayed by appear-
> ances. Tell us, then, what you think. Is it lawful to pay taxes
> to Caesar, or not?" But Jesus, aware of their malice, said,
> "Why put me to the test, you hypocrites?" (Matt. 22:15–18).

Jesus is not deceived by the flattery. He knows these men have cold,
dark hearts. Their goal is to trap Him into committing a public
relations suicide. If He says the Jews should pay their taxes, the
masses will abandon Him. If He tells the people not to pay tax, the
Romans will arrest Him. Either answer will conveniently remove
Him as a threat.

> "Show me the coin for the tax." And they brought him
> a denarius. And Jesus said to them, "Whose likeness and
> inscription is this?" They said, "Caesar's." Then he said to
> them, "Therefore render to Caesar the things that are Cae-
> sar's, and to God the things that are God's." When they
> heard it, they marveled. And they left him and went away
> (Matt. 22:19–22).

I wonder if the unspoken part of Jesus' point was lost on them.
Whose image was stamped on them? "So God created man in his
own image, in the image of God he created him; male and female he
created them" (Genesis 1:27). We are made in God's image, and we
need to render our beings to His service and ownership.

Who Is in Charge?

> For not from the east or from the west and not from the
> wilderness comes lifting up, but it is God who executes judg-
> ment, putting down one and lifting up another (Ps. 75:6–7).

While the Bible is clear that God controls governments, Satan
attempted to test Jesus, to see if, in His humanity, He would be
tempted by a corruption of temporary earthly power.

Again, the devil took him to a very high mountain and showed him all the kingdoms of the world and their glory. And he said to him, "All these I will give you, if you will fall down and worship me." Then Jesus said to him, "Be gone, Satan! For it is written, 'You shall worship the Lord your God and him only shall you serve' " (Matt. 4:8–10).

Did these earthly kingdoms belong to Satan? Were they really his to give?

The kings of the earth set themselves, and the rulers take counsel together, against the LORD and against his Anointed, saying, "Let us burst their bonds apart and cast away their cords from us." He who sits in the heavens laughs; the Lord holds them in derision. Then he will speak to them in his wrath, and terrify them in his fury, saying, "As for me, I have set my King on Zion, my holy hill." I will tell of the decree: The LORD said to me, "You are my Son; today I have begotten you. Ask of me, and I will make the nations your heritage, and the ends of the earth your possession. You shall break them with a rod of iron and dash them in pieces like a potter's vessel." Now therefore, O kings, be wise; be warned, O rulers of the earth. Serve the LORD with fear, and rejoice with trembling. Kiss the Son, lest he be angry, and you perish in the way, for his wrath is quickly kindled. Blessed are all who take refuge in him (Ps. 2:2–12).

In the Book of Daniel, King Nebuchadnezzer, the most powerful ruler on earth at that time (of the Babylonian Empire) declared the supreme rule of God over all earthly kingdoms.

At the end of the days I, Nebuchadnezzar, lifted my eyes to heaven, and my reason returned to me, and I blessed the Most High, and praised and honored him who lives forever, for his dominion is an everlasting dominion, and his kingdom endures from generation to generation; all the inhabitants of the earth are accounted as nothing, and he does according to his will among the host of heaven and among the inhabitants of the earth; and none can stay his hand or say to him, "What have you done?" At the same time my reason returned to me, and for the glory of my kingdom, my majesty and splendor returned to me. My counselors and my lords sought me, and I was established in my kingdom, and still more greatness was added to me. Now I, Nebuchadnezzar, praise and extol and honor the King of heaven, for all his works are right and his ways are just; and those who walk in pride he is able to humble (Dan. 4:34–37).

Even before the Cross, it was clear that God was not afraid of the leaders of this earth (but instead declared His authority over them all).

An Unshakeable Kingdom

It seems the power held by the Father would eventually be transferred to the Son.

> Then the seventh angel blew his trumpet, and there were loud voices in heaven, saying, "The kingdom of the world has become the kingdom of our Lord and of his Christ, and he shall reign forever and ever" (Rev. 11:15).

It also seems as though Satan has limited influence now over the earthly kingdoms of this world, but the Bible tells us that his time is short (see Rev. 12:12). When time as we have known it ends, Jesus has promised that He will give rulership of His domain to His faithful followers.

> The one who conquers and who keeps my works until the end, to him I will give authority over the nations, and he will rule them with a rod of iron, as when earthen pots are broken in pieces, even as I myself have received authority from my Father (Rev. 2:26–27).

The famous missionary to India, E. Stanley Jones (1884–1973), spoke of the unshakableness of the Kingdom of God that He had learned through his experience:

> I was in Russia in 1934, and I saw people building a civilization without God. And doing it enthusiastically. It hit me pretty hard. I needed reassurance, and so I went to my Bible one morning in Moscow, and these words arose out of the Scriptures: "Therefore let us be grateful for receiving a kingdom that cannot be shaken (Hebrews 12:28-29 RSV)." "Oh," I said, We have a kingdom that cannot be shaken. Not only will it not be shaken but it cannot be shaken. Because it's ultimate reality. The kingdom of communism is shakeable. They have to hold it together by force. The kingdom of capitalism is shakeable. When President Dwight D. Eisenhower had a heart attack, the stock market plunged $4 billion. But the kingdom of God is not shakeable. It's ultimate reality."[2]

The Gospel of the Kingdom

All throughout Jesus' ministry, He spoke constantly about the "Kingdom of God." In a final showdown, between the King of the universe, and a representative from the mightiest earthly kingdom on earth at that time, Jesus was interviewed by Pilate on what He meant by that term (king).

> So Pilate entered his headquarters again and called Jesus and said to him, "Are you the King of the Jews?" Jesus answered, "Do you say this of your own accord, or did others say it to you about me?" Pilate answered, "Am I a Jew? Your own nation and the chief priests have delivered you over to me. What have you done?" Jesus answered, "My

2. E. Stanley Jones was a Methodist evangelist, missionary to India, and founder of the Christian Ashram Movement. "Running Toward the Unshakeable Kingdom" first appeared in *Good News* magazine in 1970. It's condensed from an address he delivered at the Good News Convocation in Dallas that year.

kingdom is not of this world. If my kingdom were of this world, my servants would have been fighting, that I might not be delivered over to the Jews. But my kingdom is not from the world." Then Pilate said to him, "So you are a king?" Jesus answered, "You say that I am a king. For this purpose I was born and for this purpose I have come into the world — to bear witness to the truth. Everyone who is of the truth listens to my voice" (John 18:33–37).

Later in the trial, Jesus revealed that He was submitting to an earthly authority, but His Father still had reign over it.

The Jews answered him, "We have a law, and according to that law he ought to die because he has made himself the Son of God." When Pilate heard this statement, he was even more afraid. He entered his headquarters again and said to Jesus, "Where are you from?" But Jesus gave him no answer. So Pilate said to him, "You will not speak to me? Do you not know that I have authority to release you and authority to crucify you?" Jesus answered him, "You would have no authority over me at all unless it had been given you from above" (John 19:7–11).

The day is coming where every wicked ruler of every nation will flee in terror into caves and dens, asking the rocks and hills to fall on them and hide them from the wrath of Almighty God (Isa. 2:10, 19, 24:21; Rev. 6:15, 19:18). Every earthly king will stand before his Creator. Every knee will bow, and every tongue will confess that Jesus Christ is Lord, to the glory of God the Father (Phil. 2:10–11). Only those who have submitted to the rule and reign of Christ in this life will have the opportunity to rule and reign with Him in the next. The question for you is, "Do you have the image and name of Jesus stamped deeply on your life? Are you ready to meet Him?"

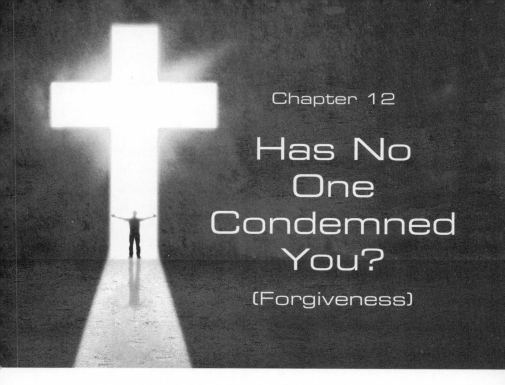

Chapter 12

Has No One Condemned You?

(Forgiveness)

H ave you ever deserved to be disciplined or punished for something you did, but never ended up receiving the retribution? I have. At least once. Usually, as a child, I didn't get away with much, but one time, I was astonishingly delivered from impending doom.

When I was about five years old, we lived in an old house in Indiana. I have a few notable memories of that house. We had an epic flood that was about three feet deep, we had a neighbor who was a grumpy preacher, and it was cold and dark in the winter. It was on one of those cold and dark Indiana mornings that I did something that can only be explained inside the mind of a five-year-old. (Whatever logic was present at that time has since escaped from my memory.)

We had a gas heater somewhere in the house, and I decided that it would be a great experiment to pee in the heater and see what would happen. What happens, I discovered, is that it fills the house with an inexplicable odor that is far less than pleasant.

As the fumes wafted throughout the house, my dad knew exactly what had happened. He had been raised in a home with four boys, and he was well acquainted with the capacity of boys to do the unbelievable. When confronted, however, I lied like a dog on a porch in the summer. There was no way I was going to own up to this one. I could tell by the look on my dad's face the he was not buying it. I was dead in the water. I was secretly making all kinds of pledges and promises to God about future devotion, and commitments to abandon my recalcitrant ways for the greener pastures of obedience and, if necessary, missionary life.

There was a saving grace, however. My dear mother. That woman has a heart of gold. She reminded my father that I had never lied before (which may have been true to that point) and that if I said I didn't do it, there was at least the slightest, remotest chance of there being another explanation and I should not be disciplined. I was SO on her side. After a time of disagreement, Mom won out! I had never been so relieved in all my life. Okay, maybe the time when I was rescued from the car trunk, but this was epic.

What troubled me later, however, was the fact that, even though I had managed to cheat the system and get away with it, I knew that God still knew the truth. I realized that, ultimately, there would be another day of reckoning, far ahead in my future. Even if no one on earth ever learned the truth, I would still stand before the judgment seat of Christ, to give an account for what I had done in this life (see 2 Cor. 5:10).

Caught in the Act

But Jesus went to the Mount of Olives. Early in the morning he came again to the temple. All the people came to him, and he sat down and taught them. The scribes and the Pharisees brought a woman who had been caught in adultery, and placing her in the midst they said to him, "Teacher, this woman has been caught in the act of adultery. Now in the Law Moses commanded us to stone such women. So what do you say?" This they said to test him, that they might have some charge to bring against him. Jesus bent down and wrote with his finger on the ground. And as they continued to ask him, he stood up and said to them, "Let him who is without sin among you be the first to throw a stone at her." And once more he bent down and wrote on the ground. But when they heard it, they went away one by one, beginning with the older ones, and Jesus was left alone with the woman standing before him. Jesus stood up and said to her, "Woman, where are they? Has no one condemned you?" She said, "No one, Lord." And Jesus said, "Neither do I condemn you; go, and from now on sin no more" (John 8:1–11).

This story is controversial on so many levels. First of all, there is even some debate about whether this account belongs in the Bible. John 7:53–8:11 is not found in some early manuscripts (but shows up in many later manuscripts). It also occasionally shows up in a different place in John's gospel. Some argue, therefore, that it was inserted later, as a fictional account, and should not be included in our modern Bibles at all. Most scholars, however, believe that it is inspired text, may have been removed (for a variety of reasons) from certain early texts, and should be included in our Bibles. Most modern English Bibles include the story, but add footnotes to reference the issue.

The Long Arm of the Law

Biblical law regarding the death penalty is as follows:

> Then you shall bring out to your gates that man or woman who has done this evil thing, and you shall stone that man or woman to death with stones. On the evidence of two witnesses or of three witnesses the one who is to die shall be put to death; a person shall not be put to death on the evidence of one witness. The hand of the witnesses shall

be first against him to put him to death, and afterward the hand of all the people. So you shall purge the evil from your midst (Deut. 17:5–7).

If a man is found lying with the wife of another man, both of them shall die, the man who lay with the woman, and the woman. So you shall purge the evil from Israel (Deut. 22:22).

During Jesus' lifetime, the land of Israel was controlled by the Roman government. Around 57 B.C., a governing body of 71 men called the Great Sanhedrin was established in Jerusalem. According to the Mishnah or *Babylonian Talmud*, capital punishment could only be carried out by a sentence made by a 23-person segment of the Sanhedrin.[1]

However, this was complicated in Jesus' lifetime, as the Jews were stripped by Caesar of their ability to carry out executions.[2] This continued until the destruction of Jerusalem in A.D. 70.[3] This loss of authority obviously would have been upsetting to the Jewish leaders. They not only lost their autonomy, but also their ability to carry out biblical law (and thereby their ability to obey God in the civil realm).

A Political Trap

There is an important historical backdrop to the story John relates to us. If the Jews carried out capital punishment, thus fulfilling their

---

1. Sanhedrin 1:4: "Capital cases are adjudicated by twenty-three."
2. A. Malamat, *A History of the Jewish People*, H.H. Ben-Sasson, editor (London: Weidenfeld and Nicolson, 1976), p. 247: "When Judea was converted into a Roman province [in 6 CE, p. 246], Jerusalem ceased to be the administrative capital of the country. The Romans moved the governmental residence and military headquarters to Caesarea. The centre of government was thus removed from Jerusalem, and the administration became increasingly based on inhabitants of the Hellenistic cities (Sebaste, Caesarea and others)."
3. *Babylonian Talmud*, Tractate (Sanhedrin, Folio 41a): "Forty years before the destruction of the Temple, the Sanhedrin were exiled and took up residence in Hanuth."

law, they would be breaking the civil law of Rome, and could potentially bring the wrath of the entire Roman Empire down on them.

This scenario is almost identical to the ethical dilemma Jesus' opponents tried to create for Him when they asked Him about Caesar's coin (see the chapter "Whose Likeness and Inscription is This?"). In that instance, if Jesus says you should obey Caesar's law and pay taxes to him, He will lose popularity with the Jewish people, most of whom despised the Roman occupation of Judea. But if Jesus says it isn't necessary to pay taxes, then He is worthy of the Roman death penalty for sedition.

Guilty or Not Guilty

So here's the deal with this particular case: It's not about the woman. She is just a pawn in the game. This is all about politics and taking Jesus down. There are so many rules broken in this case, it's not even funny. Let's consider the merits of this case.

First of all, the accused has to be caught in the act of adultery (this can't be hearsay). The mob claims she was "caught in the act." So far so good.

Second, she was caught in the act with . . . whom? Uh oh. Houston, we have a problem. Deuteronomy 22:22 insists that *both* the man *and* woman must be put to death. Where is the dude?

Third, this can only be done with two or three witnesses. There is no indication that this criteria has been met. What we have here is a mob. In the ancient Greek "Attic" law, an accusation of this sort had to be brought in writing. According to the Jewish mindset on this, a witness would be less likely to formally charge someone if they had to face them in person, and make the accusation, than if they merely had to write something on paper.

Fourth, according to the Jews' own rules, the two or three witnesses were to go to the Sanhedrin, and only the special 23-member Sanhedrin could adjudicate a death penalty. This could not be determined by a mob, just as today, proper legal procedures need to be followed.

Fifth, the accusers who had personally witnessed the crime would have been the ones to cast the first stone. If you think at all about the nature of public stoning, it was not something that was pleasant for anyone involved. You wouldn't follow through with such an accusation unless you were completely certain of a person's guilt (or you were just evil).

Writing in the Sand

Over the years, there have been countless speculations as to what Jesus wrote in the sand. The fact is, the Bible doesn't tell us. Another perhaps more important question is, why? I love how author Michael Card describes this act:

> What Jesus did that morning created a space in time that allowed the angry mob to cool down, then to hear his word, and finally to think about it, be convinced by it and respond — or not. It made time stand still. It was original. It was unexpected. It was a response to the noise and confusion and busyness all around him, yet it was not in the least tainted by the noise. Instead, Jesus' action created a frame around the silence — the kind of silence in which God speaks to the heart.[4]

Neither Do I Condemn You

In Jesus' role on earth, He did not come as a judge to condemn. God had already given His law, and established civil government to achieve that purpose.

> For God did not send his Son into the world to condemn the world, but in order that the world might be saved through him (John 3:17).

Jesus' response, calling for the one without sin to cast the first stone, was brilliant. It put the burden of execution back where it belonged

4. Michael Card, *Scribbling in the Sand: Christ and Creativity* (Downers Grove, IL: InterVarsity Press, 2002), p. 16.

— on the people who were accusing the woman. Jesus was not an eyewitness to the crime. He was not a member of the 23-man Sanhedrin. He also knew that the mob was completely ignoring both the law of God and their own man-made legal system, in order to discredit Him. He knew when silence on His part was necessary. He had no legal right to bring an accusation against the woman, and since she had not been properly sentenced by their legal system, He would be participating in a revolutionary action.

It was, in fact, this same defiance of Roman authority that was exercised by the Jews when they, in a fit of rage, ignored the ban against executions and had Stephen stoned in Acts 7:54–60.

When the mob had finally dispersed, Jesus turned to the woman, and assured her that, since the legal charges against her were dropped, He had none of His own to add. In His Messianic role, Jesus was not a judge, He was a Savior. Jesus, as a Savior, however, did not turn a blind eye to her sin. She had been let off the hook on a legal technicality. She was not condemned to death (which she may have legally deserved). So Jesus, with a pastoral warning, implores her: "Go, and from now on, sin no more."

God Made Him to be Sin Who Knew No Sin

The adulterous woman had been given a clean slate. All of us long for a chance to start over, to have the record against us expunged. It wasn't as though she was declared "Not guilty," but her sentence was not served. Isn't it ironic that standing before her was the Son of Man, who would be put to death at the false accusation of this same mob, to offer forgiveness to any who would receive Him? Through His sacrifice, we, though guilty as could be, are not sentenced. Our penalty is taken upon Jesus. Rather than condemning us, He took our penalty and died a cruel and tortuous death.

John R.W. Stott (1921–2011) describes this great exchange:

> The problem of forgiveness is constituted by the inevitable collision between divine perfection and human

rebellion, between God as he is and us as we are. The obstacle to forgiveness is neither our sin alone nor our guilt alone, but the divine reaction in love and wrath toward guilty sinners. For, although indeed "God is love," yet we have to remember that his love is "holy love," love which yearns over sinners while at the same time refusing to condone their sin. How, then, could God express his holy love — his love in forgiving sinners without compromising his holiness, and his holiness in judging sinners without frustrating his love? Confronted by human evil, how could God be true to himself as holy love? In Isaiah's words, how could he be simultaneously "a righteous God and a Savior" (Isa. 45:21)? For despite the truth that God demonstrated his righteousness by taking action to save his people, the words righteousness and salvation cannot be regarded as simple synonyms. Rather his saving initiative was compatible with, and expressive of, his righteousness. At the cross in holy love God through Christ paid the full penalty of our disobedience himself. He bore the judgment we deserve in order to bring us the forgiveness we do not deserve. On the cross divine mercy and justice were equally expressed and eternally reconciled. God's holy love was "satisfied."[5]

Because of Christ's sacrifice, we hear His words addressed to us: "Has no one condemned you?" We receive our answer in the words of Scripture.

There is therefore now no condemnation to them which are in Christ Jesus, who walk not after the flesh, but after the Spirit. For the law of the Spirit of life in Christ Jesus hath made me free from the law of sin and death (Rom. 8:1–2; KJV).

5. John Stott, *The Cross of Christ* (Downers Grove, IL: InterVarsity Press, 2012) p. 90–91.

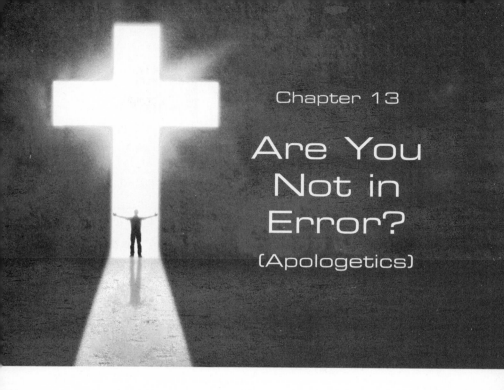

Chapter 13

Are You Not in Error?

(Apologetics)

Years ago, I was preparing to speak at a church on the topic of "Christian apologetics." The pastor introduced me enthusiastically to the congregation by telling them, "Our guest speaker tonight is speaking on the very important topic of Christian apologetics. I just want to say, I think this is a big part of what is wrong with the Church today! We've got too many people apologizing for their faith, and we aren't going to do it any longer! So, Israel, why don't you come on up here and show us from the Bible why it is wrong for Christians to be apologetic about their faith?!"

Okay, that was awkward. That wasn't what I was planning to say at all! The difficulty is, you don't know what you don't know, and even in church circles, there are so many big, fancy terms we sling around that it's easy to get lost in terminology. Especially for new Christians, or the unchurched, it is easy to be overwhelmed by terms like justification, sanctification, propitiation, transubstantiation, hermeneutics, eschatology, and, of course, the debate that is sure to split churches faster than a speeding bullet: infralapsarianism vs. supralapsarianism!

For some Christians, tossing around big theological words can be a way to seem intellectually superior to everyone else. For others, it's more a sign of being so immersed in a sub-culture that we forget to show proper consideration and inclusion to others who aren't part of our little club. In an attempt to avoid both, let me define the term for you.

The term *apologetics* actually comes from a Greek word, *apologia*. The word means, "to give a defense." It is a legal term, and it is what a trial lawyer would do when arguing on behalf of his client. So Christian apologetics is a defense for the Christian faith. This concept and the term *apologia* are found in this verse:

> But in your hearts honor Christ the Lord as holy, always being prepared to make a defense [apologia] to anyone who asks you for a reason for the hope that is in you; yet do it with gentleness and respect (1 Pet. 3:15).

If you ever try to share your faith with unbelievers, eventually you will find yourself doing apologetics, whether you call it that or not. When you present what you believe, the other person may counter with an objection, or ask a question that causes you to defend your position. When that happens, you have shifted from doing evangelism (sharing the gospel) to apologetics (defending the faith). The two are somewhat similar and they usually go hand in hand, but they are distinct.

Are You Not in Error?

One of the things we Christians assume and presuppose, as a first principle, is that all beliefs are not equal and valid. In some cultures you are taught to love your neighbor; in others, that you should eat him. I can't speak for you, but I certainly have a preference between the two!

Truth, by definition, is exclusive. To make a statement that purports to be true, you are assuming that the opposite of that statement is necessarily false. Jesus was not a relativist (someone who believes that truth is only a matter of opinion or perspective). Jesus was, despite popular current portrayals of Him, not averse to telling people they were wrong. Even emphatically wrong.

In one rather poignant debate with the Sadducees (a religious Jewish sect) on the topic of the resurrection of the dead, Jesus replied, "Are you not in error because you do not know the Scriptures or the power of God?" (Mark 12:24; NIV).

Jesus points out two key areas that had kept the Sadducees from being able to understand the truth correctly. These two areas are still a struggle for Christians today: biblical literacy and experiencing the power of God in their personal lives.

Biblical Literacy

Eighty-eight percent of adults in America own a Bible. Twenty-six percent of Americans have never read the Bible at all, and only 13 percent read it several times a week. The younger you are, the less likely you are to read the Bible. Of those who read the Bible, only 43 percent give any significant thought to how they can apply it to their lives, and only 31 percent of evangelicals are considered to be "highly knowledgeable" about the Bible.[1]

Even though many people don't know what the Bible actually teaches, that hasn't stopped them from having an opinion on it (and often a very negative one!). I guess this should not surprise us. Jude 1:10 reveals that even in the first century people would curse things of the Lord they didn't understand.

Ironically, the Sadducees were actually pretty devout Bible scholars. They comprised one-half of the Jewish Sanhedrin (along with the Pharisees), and as such, the two groups served as a religious equivalent to our Republicans and Democrats.

A major problem with the Sadducees, as with most of us, was their bias. They had certain preconceived ideas, which they believed to be true, that shaped their viewpoint before the conversation had

---

1. http://www.americanbible.org/uploads/content/state-of-the-bible-data-analy-sis-american-bible-society-2014.pdf.

even begun. Our presuppositions often act as colored lenses that shade and tint the way we understand what we hear and read.

So one problem would be not reading the Bible, and therefore being ignorant of its content. Another would be reading it with a predisposition, assuming certain things must be true (or cannot be true) and interpreting the text accordingly. The Sadducees had determined ahead of time that there was no such thing as a resurrection of the dead, so any passage of Scripture that seemed to suggest that, they would quickly dismiss, or explain it away.

Many Christians in our day do this with origins. They assume, because of preconceived ideas they have from their science textbooks, that the earth must be billions of years old. Therefore, when they read the Bible, they are always trying to force the text to fit their bias.

Exegesis

The proper approach to understanding the Bible is to read the text, and determine its meaning from what it actually says. This is called "exegesis."

Eisegesis

The wrong way to approach Bible study is to approach the text with a prior set of beliefs and assumptions, and then attempt to manipulate, or alter, the text to conform to your views.

The Call for Christian Apologetics

There is a need for Christians who know the Scriptures and have the ability to defend them. In God's Word, both Jesus and Paul are revealed to have utilized apologetics in ministry.

> For the weapons of our warfare are not of the flesh but have divine power to destroy strongholds. We destroy arguments and every lofty opinion raised against the knowledge of God, and take every thought captive to obey Christ (2 Cor. 10:4–5).

Christian apologetics continued in the second century, after the Apostles, with a guy named Justin (c. A.D. 100–165). He was raised as a heathen Greek living in a Jewish culture. After being steeped in Stoic, Platonic, and other pagan Greek philosophies, he became a follower of Christ in A.D. 132. He had considered himself to be a staunch follower of Plato, but he was compelled to look into the claims of Christ when he saw the peaceful and joyful way that Christians embraced being put to death for their beliefs.

Coming from this classical philosophical background, he saw the need to communicate the truth of the gospel to the academics and intellectuals of his day. His initial defense was not against the hardened atheists, as is often the role of Christian apologists today, but instead he had to demonstrate that Christianity was not itself atheistic! Because Christians didn't embrace the polytheism (belief in many gods) of the Romans, they were highly despised and misrepresented. Rumors were even started that these Christians were cannibals (because of their belief in the bread and cup in communion representing the body and blood of Jesus).

His essay, *First Apology*, was written to the Emperor Antoninus Pius (emperor from A.D. 138 to 161) to help him understand Christianity's true tenets, and persuade him to stop persecuting its adherents. He also sent copies to Antoninus' two sons, Verissimus the Philosopher, and Lucius the Philosopher. The *Second Apology* was written to the Roman Senate for the same purpose. Far from hiding in the catacombs, Justin felt compelled to take the truth of the gospel to the very gates of antagonism and bigotry against his faith.

As one might expect, his brave defense of the gospel did not come without a price. Around 165 B.C., Justin, with six companions — Chariton, Charito, Evelpostos, Pæon, Hierax, and Liberianos — was condemned to death by the Roman prefect Rusticus. Here is an account of their sentence:

> The Prefect Rusticus says: "Approach and sacrifice, all of you, to the gods." Justin says: "No one in his right mind

gives up piety for impiety." The Prefect Rusticus says: "If you do not obey, you will be tortured without mercy." Justin replies: "That is our desire, to be tortured for our Lord, Jesus Christ, and so to be saved, for that will give us salvation and firm confidence at the more terrible universal tribunal of our Lord and Saviour." And all the martyrs said: "Do as you wish; for we are Christians, and we do not sacrifice to idols." The Prefect Rusticus read the sentence: "Those who do not wish to sacrifice to the gods and to obey the emperor will be scourged and beheaded according to the laws." The holy martyrs glorifying God betook themselves to the customary place, where they were beheaded and consummated their martyrdom confessing their Saviour.[2]

After being beheaded for his faith, he was given the name "Justin Martyr" and became an example not only for the many Christian apologists who would come after him, but the scores of martyrs as well.

Heart and Mind

The second part of Jesus' critique of the Sadducees was that they didn't have an experiential understanding of, and relationship with, the power of God. This is of utmost importance to the believer.

As I have met thousands of Christians over my lifetime, I have observed that many tend to land in one ditch or the other. Some have a very emotional experience in their conversion (nothing at all wrong with that!), which often leads to a very subjective and personal relationship with Christ that is based on strong emotions and/or spiritual connection. You'll never catch them reading theological books because, in their view, that is just dry, dead religion.

Paul warns against being an anti-intellectual Christian: "For I bear them witness that they have a zeal for God, but not according to knowledge" (Rom. 10:2).

---

2. "Acta SS.," April, II, 104–19; Otto, "Corpus Apologetarum," III, Jena, 1879, 266–78; P.G., VI, 1565–72

Others tend to be more academic and cerebral in their approach to Christianity. For them, it's not about feelings, or experiences; it's about doctrine, creeds, written confessions of the Church, and objective truth. For some, Christianity is a very intellectual process. They believe that being a Christian is all about a mental assent to a list of core teachings.

Jesus said of the Pharisees and scribes, who took this view in Jesus' day, "This people honors me with their lips, but their heart is far from me; in vain do they worship me, teaching as doctrines the commandments of men" (Matt. 15:8–9).

Instead of making a false dichotomy between these two concepts, Jesus taught an integration of our entire being in worship to God: "You shall love the Lord your God with all your heart and with all your soul and with all your strength and with all your mind, and your neighbor as yourself" (Luke 10:27).

God is spirit, and those who worship him must worship in spirit and truth (John 4:24).

There is always a context to didactic truth. It is always embodied and lived out in the context of relationships, which require whole-hearted love. Ephesians 4:15 tells us of our need to "speak the truth in love."

If one does not daily experience the power of God, working in and through our lives, transforming us from the inside out, intellectual beliefs about God can become a weapon with which we bludgeon our fellow man, and alienate him from Christ.

I have known a number of Christian apologists who have great arguments defending the historicity of the Resurrection, or can give a great defense for biblical creation, or logical arguments against atheism, but the individuals themselves are arrogant, and rude to other people, looking down on others who are not as intelligent or well-read as they are. This is surely not the heart of Christ.

I love how Christian apologist Ravi Zacharias explains the balance we need: "This is one of the most defining differences between an apologist who is merely interested in arguments and an apologist who knows God in a clear and personal walk with him. To the skeptic, to say that prayer is more about the lordship of Christ than it is about getting answers may seem at first blush to be evasive, but it is not. It is in keeping with the worldview that God's presence is a felt presence and must be pursued with diligence — and it is precisely what 'ask, seek, and knock' means."[3]

Jesus' question calls out to us today. In what ways are we ignorant of the Scriptures? How can we apply ourselves more diligently to the pursuit of this goal: "Do your best to present yourself to God as one approved, a worker who has no need to be ashamed, rightly handling the word of truth" (2 Tim. 2:15)?

In what ways are we deficient of the power of God in our lives? Is the Holy Spirit active and alive in conforming us daily into the image of Christ? Are we growing equally in both our knowledge of and love for Jesus? Are we growing in love toward others? Do we have an increasing burden for the souls of those who don't know Christ? We need to know God before we can truly love Him. We need to know the Bible before we can obey it. We don't need to be in a ditch on one side or the other. We need hearts, souls, and minds, fully engaged in the passionate pursuit of God's love, Spirit, and truth.

---

3. Ravi Zacharias, *Has Christianity Failed You?* (Grand Rapids, MI: Zondervan, 2010), p. 157–158.

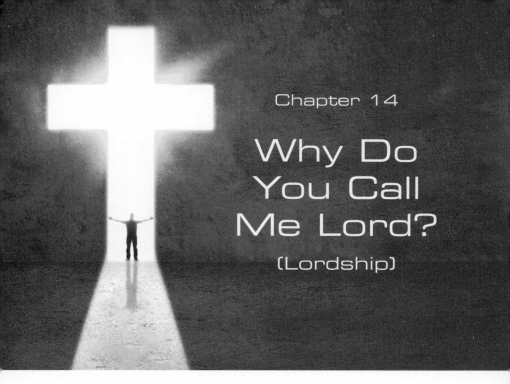

Chapter 14

Why Do You Call Me Lord?

(Lordship)

I was raised in the evangelical sub-culture. That can be both good and bad. There is much that I appreciate about the evangelical church world, and perhaps just as much that I don't. C.S. Lewis once said that the difficulty we often have in relating to non-Christians is that they usually assume we are Christians because we like church, or prefer to spend time with Christians or enjoy their sub-culture, or something of that sort. That certainly isn't the reason I'm a Christian! The difficulty we find is in convincing people that the reason we are Christians is that we believe it to be true![1]

Since the mid-19th century in particular, evangelicalism has undergone a tremendous metamorphosis, from a modernist world-view, to a postmodern one. In the worldview of modernism,[2] people believed in absolutes, rules, standards, and fixed reference points for life. Under postmodernity, everything is negotiable. There are no

1. A topic discussed in *God in the Dock*, by C.S. Lewis, originally published in 1971.
2. Modernism is a worldview, or way of seeing life, that was dominant in Western culture between about 1859 and 1959.

rules (except "don't judge anyone" and "don't make rules"). There is no hierarchy. (Everything is level, truth is whatever works for you, no one should ever make claims of certainty, no one way is right, etc.)

The postmodern worldview has permeated the Church in the West. Rather than the Church impacting and changing culture, the reverse has been true.

The concepts of "easy believism" or "cheap grace" are so commonly accepted in most churches today that the majority of Christians believe they are biblical and normal. This is the concept that Jesus wants you to be happy and healthy, and He'll help you achieve your highest potential in life. He loves you and has a wonderful plan for your life. All you have to do to become a Christian and go to heaven is to say a simple prayer and ask Jesus into your heart to be your personal Savior. Sound familiar? Well, it wouldn't surprise me, because that is what is promoted today as "the gospel."

The problem is, this is not the message that was proclaimed by Jesus or the disciples. Far from it. Not only do you never find most of those clichés in the Bible, you don't even find those general concepts being promoted (at least not when you read the message of the gospel as a whole). The neutered "gospel" of today says little to nothing about repentance, obedience, discipleship, or Lordship. In fact, any teaching on obeying Christ today will be labeled by most church-goers as being "legalistic." They will accuse you of trying to "earn your salvation."

I grew up hearing, from the pulpit, that God's grace was like a blanket God would throw over your sin so that He didn't see it any more. It was said that when God looked at you, He couldn't even see the sins you were presently committing, but instead, all He could see was the blood of Jesus. Ever heard that? It's rampant. It's all over Christian broadcasting and in Christian teaching. It's just not in the Bible.

Why Do You Not Do What I Tell You?

Jesus confronted this mentality in His day as well. "Why do you call me 'Lord, Lord,' and not do what I tell you?" (Luke 6:46). He went on to say that the person who listens to Jesus' teaching, but doesn't obey it, is like a fool who builds his house on shifting sand. Everything that man (or woman) is building on, and trusting in, will soon collapse.

I believe this question is extremely relevant for Christians today. Many people claim to belong to Jesus, but they live like the devil.

Cheap Grace

When I was about 21 years old, I met a man who had a radical impact on my life. He seemed to be seeing many of the same things I was seeing regarding the condition of the Church and Jesus' radical call of obedience and discipleship. We didn't actually "meet" though, because this guy had died 30 years before I was born. His name was Dietrich Bonhoeffer. Born in 1906, he was a young German pastor who had been put to death by the Nazis in 1945 for his role in trying to bring down the Third Reich. I "met" him through the pages of his epic book, *The Cost of Discipleship*.

This devoted follower of Jesus wrote in 1937 (as Hitler was rising to power): "Cheap grace (is) the grace which amounts to the justification of sin without the justification of the sinner who departs from sin and from whom sin departs. Cheap grace is not the kind of forgiveness of sin which frees us from the toils of sin. Cheap grace is the grace we bestow on ourselves. Cheap grace is the preaching of forgiveness without requiring repentance, baptism without church discipline, Communion without confession, absolution without personal confession. Cheap grace is grace without discipleship, grace without the cross, grace without Jesus, living and incarnate."[3]

> "Not everyone who says to me, 'Lord, Lord,' will enter the kingdom of heaven, but the one who does the will of my Father who is in heaven" (Matt. 7:21).

---

3. Dietrich Bonhoeffer, *The Cost of Discipleship* (New York, NY: Macmillian, 1963), p.47.

According to Jesus, true believers will exhibit actions that are consistent with their claim of having been regenerated by the Holy Spirit. "If you love me, you will keep my commandments" (John 14:15).

If You Love Jesus, You Will Obey

"Whoever has my commandments and keeps them, he it is who loves me. And he who loves me will be loved by my Father, and I will love him and manifest myself to him." Judas (not Iscariot) said to him, "Lord, how is it that you will manifest yourself to us, and not to the world?" Jesus answered him, "If anyone loves me, he will keep my word, and my Father will love him, and we will come to him and make our home with him. Whoever does not love me does not keep my words. And the word that you hear is not mine but the Father's who sent me" (John 14:21–24).

"If you keep my commandments, you will abide in my love, just as I have kept my Father's commandments and abide in his love" (John 15:10).

But be doers of the word, and not hearers only, deceiving yourselves (James 1:22).

True Saving Faith Creates Obedience

We don't obey God's commands in an attempt to try to earn God's grace, or do good works to gain salvation. But rather, because we have received the unmerited favor of God, it creates in us a desire to please God and serve Him with our lives.

I appeal to you therefore, brothers, by the mercies of God, to present your bodies as a living sacrifice, holy and acceptable to God, which is your spiritual worship (Rom. 12:1).

For by grace you have been saved through faith. And this is not your own doing; it is the gift of God, not a result of works, so that no one may boast. For we are his workmanship, created in Christ Jesus for good works, which God prepared beforehand, that we should walk in them (Eph. 2:8–10).

> What good is it, my brothers, if someone says he has faith but does not have works? Can that faith save him? . . . So also faith by itself, if it does not have works, is dead. But someone will say, "You have faith and I have works." Show me your faith apart from your works, and I will show you my faith by my works. . . . Do you want to be shown, you foolish person, that faith apart from works is useless? . . . You see that faith was active along with his works, and faith was completed by his works. . . . You see that a person is justified by works and not by faith alone (James 2:14–24).

Obedience is one of the tests that John outlines in his epistle that help us to make our calling and election sure.

> And by this we know that we have come to know him, if we keep his commandments. Whoever says "I know him" but does not keep his commandments is a liar, and the truth is not in him, but whoever keeps his word, in him truly the love of God is perfected. By this we may know that we are in him: whoever says he abides in him ought to walk in the same way in which he walked (1 John 2:3–6).

Jesus Has Walked in Our Shoes

A good leader will never tell his followers to do things that he won't do. Great leaders always lead by example. They don't just tell you *what* to do: they demonstrate *how* to do it. That is what Jesus did for us.

> Although he was a son, he learned obedience through what he suffered. And being made perfect, he became the source of eternal salvation to all who obey him (Heb. 5:8–9).

For to this you have been called, because Christ also suffered for you, leaving you an example, so that you might follow in his steps. He committed no sin, neither was deceit found in his mouth (1 Pet. 2:21–22).

Obedience is a Prerequisite for Answered Prayer

And whatever we ask we receive from him, because we keep his commandments and do what pleases him. And this is his commandment, that we believe in the name of his Son Jesus Christ and love one another, just as he has commanded us. Whoever keeps his commandments abides in God, and God in him. And by this we know that he abides in us, by the Spirit whom he has given us (1 John 3:22–24).

What Hinders Obedience?

In his book, *With Christ in the School of Obedience*, Andrew Murray (1828–1917) explains why we resist the concept of obedience as a requirement for the Christian.

Self is the root of all lack of love and obedience. Our Lord called His disciple to deny himself and to take up his cross; to forsake all, to hate and lose his own life, to humble himself and become the servant of all. He did so, because self, self-will, self-pleasing, self-seeking, is simply the source of all sin.[4]

The fact is, someone is always going to be king, or lord. As Bob Dylan once sang, "It may be the devil, it may be the Lord, but you're gonna have to serve somebody."[5] Sometimes, we just want the king of the universe to be us!

---

4. Andrew Murray, *With Christ in the School of Obedience*, originally published in 1898, https://books.google.com/books?id=7B4ySHSVt-B0C&printsec=frontcover&dq=https://books.google.com/books?isbn%3D1610251407&hl=en&sa=X&ei=3HGkVIvQJIX8yQShq4G-gAw&ved=0CDIQ6AEwAA#v=onepage&q&f=false

5. Lyrics by Bob Dylan, from the *Slow Train Coming* album, Copyright © 1979 by Special Rider Music.

Jesus has not allowed us the option of dual citizenship between the kingdom of self and Kingdom of God. "No one can serve two masters, for either he will hate the one and love the other, or he will be devoted to the one and despise the other" (Matt. 6:24).

The question to each of us is, "Why do you call me 'Lord'?" Is it simply because we want to be saved from hell? Is it because we think Jesus will make us healthy, wealthy, and wise? Is it because we were raised in a Christian sub-culture, and don't want to lose face with our family and friends? Or is it because we believe Jesus' claims to be God in the flesh, and we desire to thank Him for His sacrifice by loving and serving Him all of our days, because He is worthy? Why do you call Him "Lord"?

Chapter 15

Are You Still Sleeping?

(Prayer)

Ever have a preacher who was a frustrated comedian? Yeah . . . not fun. I did too. It caused me to become an object lesson in a rather conspicuous way. I'm thinking back to the days when churches still had evening services. Seriously. They used to do that. There was not only Sunday morning service, there was *also* a Sunday night service and a Wednesday night prayer meeting. But, of course, all of that was before lattes, ESVs, hipster glasses, and skinny jeans. Yeah . . . I know, I'm old.

Well, at some of those evening services, especially in the winter when the days were shortened and it got dark early, I'd get sleepy. Hey, I was just a kid. I had an excuse! But this prankster pastor would often suddenly burst into a rousing a cappella rendition of the song, based on Isaiah 52:1, "Awake O Israel: Put off Thy Slumber!" (In case the subtlety is too much here, let me remind you that my name bears a striking resemblance to a small Middle Eastern country that is referenced a lot in the Bible!) I would suddenly jolt awake, only to realize that all of the people in the congregation were looking at me . . . and chuckling. This goes to prove (for those who haven't figured it out yet) that the church people I grew up with were a little off!

What is ironic is that I have now had the blessing of being on the other side of the pulpit for many years. As an itinerant speaker, I've been privileged to speak at hundreds of conferences and churches around the country. It's so funny to watch people, who know they shouldn't be sleeping, fighting off slumber while you are speaking. As a speaker, I'm the kind of guy who makes it my ambition to do whatever is necessary to keep my listeners awake! If that involves walking over to you and bringing you up on stage as an object lesson, then so be it! (Let this be a warning to you if you ever get to hear me speak in person!)

Many years ago, before a church service where I was the guest speaker, I asked the pastor, "Does it bother you when people in your congregation fall asleep when you are preaching?"

"No, it doesn't bother me at all," he answered, with a straight face. I waited for the punch line. There was none. "The people in my church work hard," he continued. "They have children to raise, busy work schedules, lots of stresses. Some work on farms and rise at 4:00 a.m. to milk the cows. Others work in hospitals or factories where they are on the night shift. I'm amazed that some of them even make it to the service! If they are able to unwind from all of the pressure, and simply rest their souls for a half an hour, I sometimes think a nap might be the best thing for them at that point."

I was amazed by his humility and self-deprecating service to his flock, even if I did wonder how much subconscious benefit they were getting from this process if it happened every week! I decided then and there that I needed to get over this pressure that I feel to keep people interested in my message. I had always felt that if people were falling asleep, I wasn't communicating effectively and needed to up my game. So with a new, recalibrated vision, I endeavored to preach without thought as to whether or not it kept my audience awake. Within three minutes of beginning my sermon, that very pastor with whom I had been talking fell sound asleep. I mean, drop dead, stone cold . . . out! When they are snoring, it's not a moment of prayer and meditation! I'm just sayin'!

I learned that I am not as humble and accommodating as that pastor. It still concerns me when I am speaking and people fall asleep. I still feel like I'm boring them, and I do my best to keep them alert!

Why is it so hard for us to pay attention once we are finally still and quiet? When the hectic pace of life backs off just a touch, we are so exhausted that it's hard for us to pray or to read the Word.

Some friends of mine are Amish Christians, and they were telling me about their bishop, who doesn't believe in being "born again." When my friend confronted him about consistently falling asleep every time one of their ministers preaches, the bishop replied, "The Word of God is soothing. It calms you. When you read a novel, it gets you all excited and worked up, but when you read the Bible or try to pray, you fall asleep. That's how it works. It's soothing." My friend didn't buy that explanation. I don't either. But it does seem that there is a battle that goes on sometimes between our bodies, which are subject to weariness, and our souls that desperately need to be fed.

Habits of Prayer

The prophet Daniel prayed three times a day to God (Dan. 6:10). Charles Spurgeon (1834–1892) advocated the practice of having both morning and evening prayers. Jesus prayed early in the morning, before sunrise (Mark 1:35), in the evening (Matt. 14:23), and even all through the night (Luke 6:12). The Apostles continually devoted themselves to prayer (Acts 1:19). Paul said we should pray at all times and on every occasion in the power of the Holy Spirit (Eph. 6:18). Peter encouraged us to continually maintain a sober spirit for the purpose of prayer (1 Pet. 4:7).

E.M. Bounds (1835–1913), one of the greatest writers on the topic of prayer, records the following accounts of just a few of the great praying men of the past:

The great Scottish minister, Robert Murray McCheyne (1813–1843), tells about his discipline of morning prayers: "I ought to pray before seeing anyone. Often when I sleep long, or meet with others early, it is eleven or twelve o'clock before I begin secret prayer. This is a wretched system. It is unscriptural. Christ arose before day and went into a solitary place. David says: 'Early will I seek thee'; 'Thou shalt early hear my voice.' Family loses much of its power and sweetness, and I can do no good to those who come to seek from me. The conscience feels guilty, the soul unfed, the lamp untrimmed. Then when in secret prayer, the soul is often out of tune, I feel it is far better to begin with God — to see His face first, to get my soul near Him before it is near another."[1]

John Wesley (1703–1791) rose at 4:00 a.m. consistently for over 60 years for morning prayers.

Martin Luther (1483–1546) said, "If I fail to spend two hours in prayer each morning, the devil gets the victory through the day. I have so much business I cannot get on without spending three hours daily in prayer."

Francis Asbury (1745–1816) shared, "I purpose to rise at four o'clock as often as I can and spend two hours in prayer and meditation."

Edward Payson (1783–1827), a Congregational minister, prayed so many hours on his knees that he wore grooves in his wood floor boards!

George Whitefield (1714–1770) said, "Whole days and weeks have I spent prostrate on the ground in silent or vocal prayer."

Of all of the spiritual disciplines, prayer is the most difficult for me. However, I love reading the writings of, and stories about, great men of prayer, like A.W. Tozer, Andrew Murray, Leonard

---

1. E.M. Bounds, *The Complete Works of E.M. Bound on Prayer*. http://www.amazon.com/Complete-Bounds-Prayer-Contents-Annotated-ebook/dp/B004Z4I-YA0/.

Ravenhill, John "Praying" Hyde, George Müller, E.M. Bounds, etc. It encourages me to spend less time in frivolous pursuits and more time in fellowship and intercession with my Father.

Watch and Pray

At Jesus' darkest hour, when the trial and eventual crucifixion was only hours away, Jesus slipped away to a quiet place so He could pray and seek the Father. If there was ever a time when He could have used a team of supporters willing to do intercessory prayer on His behalf, it was now.

> And they went to a place called Gethsemane. And he said to his disciples, "Sit here while I pray." And he took with him Peter and James and John, and began to be greatly distressed and troubled. And he said to them, "My soul is very sorrowful, even to death. Remain here and watch." And going a little farther, he fell on the ground and prayed that, if it were possible, the hour might pass from him. And he said, "Abba, Father, all things are possible for you. Remove this cup from me. Yet not what I will, but what you will." And he came and found them sleeping, and he said to Peter, "Simon, are you asleep? Could you not watch one hour?" (Mark 14:32–37).

This question was surely in response to the braggadocio claims Peter and the others had made, literally right before they left for the garden.

> Peter said to him, "Even though they all fall away, I will not." And Jesus said to him, "Truly, I tell you, this very night, before the rooster crows twice, you will deny me three times." But he said emphatically, "If I must die with you, I will not deny you." And they all said the same (Mark 14:29–31).

The Bible tells us to put "no confidence in the flesh" (Phil. 3:3). Jesus always relied entirely on the empowerment of the Holy Spirit to do the will of the Father (see Acts 10:38). He tried to teach His disciples to do the same.

> "Watch and pray that you may not enter into temptation. The spirit indeed is willing, but the flesh is weak." And again he went away and prayed, saying the same words. And again he came and found them sleeping, for their eyes were very heavy, and they did not know what to answer him. And he came the third time and said to them, "Are you still sleeping and taking your rest? It is enough; the hour has come. The Son of Man is betrayed into the hands of sinners. Rise, let us be going; see, my betrayer is at hand" (Mark 14:38–42).

The disciples should not have been caught off guard because Jesus had warned the disciples in advance that such a battle was soon to emerge. "But stay awake at all times, praying that you may have strength to escape all these things that are going to take place, and to stand before the Son of Man" (Luke 21:36).

How to Pray

Long before the day of His arrest, Jesus had established a discipline of prayer as an example to His disciples. In what has become known as "The Lord's Prayer," Jesus outlined a pattern for prayer. Luke 11:1 tells us that Jesus gave them this instruction from a request by one of His disciples seeking to learn how to pray, just as John the Baptist's disciples had learned prayer from their mentor.

> And when you pray, you must not be like the hypocrites. For they love to stand and pray in the synagogues and at the street corners, that they may be seen by others. Truly, I say to you, they have received their reward. But when you pray, go into your room and shut the door and

pray to your Father who is in secret. And your Father who sees in secret will reward you. And when you pray, do not heap up empty phrases as the Gentiles do, for they think that they will be heard for their many words. Do not be like them, for your Father knows what you need before you ask him. Pray then like this: "Our Father in heaven, hallowed be your name. Your kingdom come, your will be done, on earth as it is in heaven. Give us this day our daily bread, and forgive us our debts, as we also have forgiven our debtors. And lead us not into temptation, but deliver us from evil" (Matt. 6:5–13).

There are several notable details that stand out from this lesson.

1. Jesus assumes that we will pray. He says, "When you pray . . ." not "If you pray . . ." (Eph. 6:18; 1 Thess. 5:17).
2. Prayer is between you and God; it's not to be used to impress others (Luke 18:9–14).
3. Prayer does not need to be elaborate and pompous, but instead, it should be heartfelt (Eccles. 5:2).
4. God already knows our needs, but He instructs us to ask Him (Matt. 7:7–8, James 4:2–3).
5. We pray "Our Father" to remember we have intimate access to God. Also, we unite in prayer in the Body of Christ as a family (Matt. 18:19).
6. All prayer begins with the realization that God is infinitely holy (and therefore all He does is just and right) (Gen. 18:25; Ps. 25:10).
7. God's Kingdom, and His will being done in and through our lives, is our primary desire, not building "our own kingdom." Jesus emulated this in His prayer in the garden, "Not my will, but yours, be done" (Luke 22:42).
8. It is legitimate to ask God to meet our basic necessities (1 Tim. 6:8–10).

9. The things we desire for ourselves (forgiveness, blessing, etc.), we should desire for others (Matt. 6:14–15, 18:34–35; Rom. 12:14).
10. We have an enemy. Prayer is one of the ways we battle against him and gain victory over sin (Eph. 6:10–18; James 5:16).

Jesus Prayed for His Disciples

In John 17, Jesus set an example for His disciples by interceding for them. If Jesus were to pray for you (and we know He does — Heb. 7:25), what do you think He would pray? In this passage, Jesus asks the Father for the following things on our behalf:

1. v. 3: That we might know God and His son, Jesus. (Knowledge of God)
2. v. 11: That we would be kept in the Father's name. (Security)
3. v. 13: That Jesus' joy would be fulfilled in us. (Joy)
4. v. 15: That we would be kept from the Evil One. (Deliverance)
5. v. 17: That we would be sanctified in the Truth, which is the Word of God. (Sanctification)
6. v. 21: That we would be one, even as Jesus and the Father are one. (Unity)
7. v. 21: That we would be united with the Father and Son. (Redemption)
8. v. 21: That the world may believe through our unity with God and each other. (Evangelism)
9. v. 24: That we could be where Jesus is. (Eternal Life)
10. v. 24: That we may see Jesus' glory. (Glorification)

And lest you think that I'm stretching things a bit when I suggest that Jesus may pray these same things for you, listen to His own words: "I do not ask for these only, but also for those who will believe in me through their word" (John 17:20).

The Glory and Honor Due Christ

Why did Jesus pray these things for His disciples (including us)? I believe this verse explains the heart behind not only Jesus' prayers, but His willingness to go to the Cross.

> "Father, I desire that they also, whom you have given me, may be with me where I am, to see my glory that you have given me because you loved me before the foundation of the world" (John 17:24).

It was to the honor of the Father and the glorification of Himself that He went to the Cross (see Heb. 12:2). Through His death, He redeemed that which had been corrupted by the Fall. His Kingdom and eternal reign would result from His suffering and shed blood. Mankind would be bought back. Death and sin would be defeated. This was the will of the Father, and it became the will of the Son as well.

As we become one with the Father and the Son, this burden will become ours as well. Our prayers will no longer be focused on our selfish desires and petty whims and wishes. Instead, we will increasingly pray for the glory of the Father to be demonstrated through the Son, that God's perfect will for His Kingdom would be accomplished and implemented here on this earth, just as it is perfectly carried out currently in heaven. We will pray that those held captive to the enemy will be set free, and that Jesus will receive the reward due His suffering.

> And they sang a new song, saying: "You are worthy to take the scroll and to open its seals, because you were slain, and with your blood you purchased for God persons from every tribe and language and people and nation" (Rev. 5:9; NIV).

Someday, in the heavenly Kingdom, all of these battles, these sufferings, these temptations, and fleshly impulses will be laid aside. All of the things we have prayed for, worked for, and longed for, will be restored and completed. There will be no need for prayer in heaven; instead, we will worship with complete freedom. It is then, and only then, we can completely rest.

Then the King will say to those on his right, "Come, you who are blessed by my Father, inherit the kingdom prepared for you from the foundation of the world" (Matt. 25:34).

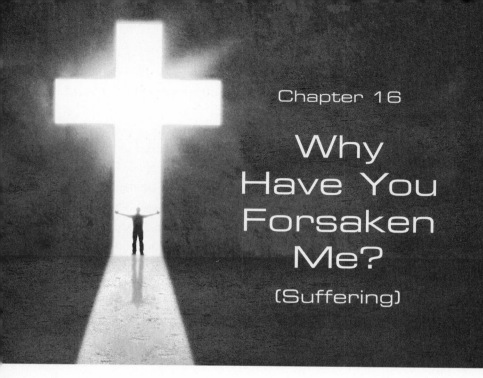

Chapter 16

Why Have You Forsaken Me?

(Suffering)

On a scale of 1 to 10, with ten being the worst pain you have ever experienced in your life, what is your current level of pain? If you have ever been in a hospital recovering from a surgery, you have likely heard this question. Physical agony is hard enough to deal with, but emotional hurts can be far worse.

Many of us don't like to talk about our grief. It's intensely personal, so we often internalize it and keep it private. We sometimes assume that others won't be able to relate to our experiences, or they would judge us harshly if they knew what we've been through. What we forget is that if you have lived life for any length of time, you have been hurt by the cruelty of the world in which we live.

My Journey

When I was a boy, from the age of 6 through 15, I lived with a stepfather who was extremely physically, verbally, and psychologically abusive. Those years are so pivotal to establishing your sense of identity and manhood. When I was 15, my mom moved my five sisters and myself across the country, and we attempted to start a new life away from my stepfather.

One Sunday morning shortly after our move, I was sitting in a church service, having my own personal communication with God. For as long as I could remember, I had always believed all of the essential doctrines of the Christian faith. I believed that God created everything (in six literal, 24-hour days); that the Bible was the inspired, infallible Word of God; that Jesus was the Son of God, was born of a virgin, died for our sins, bodily rose again from the dead in three days, etc.

Theology proper wasn't really a problem for me at that moment. I believed in the omniscience, omnipresence, and omnipotence of God. The thing that I was struggling with was believing that God really cared about me. "God, I believe that You know all things and that You are all-powerful. I get that. What I don't understand is why, given those factors, You have allowed the things that have happened in my life. Isn't that important to You? Don't You love me?"

The heavens were silent, and God seemed a million miles away.

For anyone who has ever found themselves at the end of their emotional rope, hanging on for dear life, hoping they don't let go, remember that our Lord Himself experienced this sense of alienation and isolation as well.

Forsaken by God?

If anyone in the universe ever had a proper theology of God, it would have been Jesus. Since the beginning of time, He had shared fellowship with the Godhead. He knew God, because He was God!

And yet, in His humanity, in His suffering on the Cross, Jesus cried out in agony, screaming these spine-chilling words: "My God, my God, why have you forsaken me?" (Matt. 27:46).

How was it possible for God to be forsaken by God? Did Jesus not understand that this sacrifice of His life was God's plan for redemption, to purchase back sinful humans and reconcile them to God? Of course He did. He had already wrestled this out during His prayers in the Garden of Gethsemane.

Two Perspectives

Fulfillment of Prophecy

The first perspective for us to remember is that Jesus was not merely uttering a guttural reaction to His present condition. On the contrary, in the midst of the most intense human pain imaginable, Jesus was laser-focused on the task at hand.

> "My God, my God, why have you forsaken me? Why are you so far from saving me, from the words of my groaning?" (Ps. 22:1).

The rest of Psalm 22 reveals that Jesus was fulfilling a Messianic prophecy spoken by King David. One thousand years before the birth of Christ, the Holy Spirit inspired David to describe the death of Jesus: being scorned, despised, and mocked; experiencing congestive heart failure; being thirsty; being surrounded by Gentiles; His hands and feet being pierced (it is important to note that the cruel method of crucifixion implemented by the Romans wasn't a practice in David's day); and even the casting of lots for His clothes. All of this was foretold in a way that could have only been fulfilled by Jesus' unique death. Jesus' quotation of this Psalm was one more step toward the completion of His mission.

So on one level, Jesus was not asking this question for His own benefit, but rather for His hearers, and for us, to understand that Jesus was the Messiah, and He was completing the words of prophecy that had been declared about His death.

Emotional Response

The other equally valid perspective is to realize that Jesus experienced the full weight of the sensations that accompanied His humanity. Life is not merely a daily exercise of mind over matter. We feel, we hurt, we are tempted, and we experience the full panoply of emotions and temptations that are intrinsic to our human experience.

> For we do not have a high priest who is unable to sympathize with our weaknesses, but one who in every respect has been tempted as we are, yet without sin (Heb. 4:15).

We must remember that Jesus had always experienced perfect fellowship with the Father, but for the first time, on the Cross, He became the object of God's wrath. Jesus' agony was not merely because of His excruciating physical pain (note: the word "excruciating" comes from the same root word as "crucifixion"), but also from the pain of being crushed by the Father, taking our sin upon Himself, and feeling the full weight of God's hatred of sin directed toward Him on the Cross.

> Yet it was the will of the LORD to crush him; he has put him to grief; when his soul makes an offering for guilt (Is. 53:10).

> For our sake he made him to be sin who knew no sin, so that in him we might become the righteousness of God (2 Cor. 5:21).

> Christ redeemed us from the curse of the law by becoming a curse for us — for it is written, "Cursed is everyone who is hanged on a tree" (Gal. 3:13).

Jesus embraced the penalty that we deserved by taking our place upon the Cross. He did this so that He could become our High Priest and advocate before the Father. He experienced being forsaken by the Father so that we would never have to.

Love Allows Suffering

There are two things that we always need to remember about God. First, God is infinitely powerful and wise. Second, He always acts in love to achieve what is best in the end.

One thing God has spoken, two things I have heard: "Power belongs to you, God, and with you, Lord, is unfailing love" (Ps. 62:11–12; NIV).

If our theology only emphasized the strength of God, or the knowledge of God, we might imagine Him to be capricious or cruel. If we only know Him to be loving, we might conclude that He is inept or unable to rise to our defense. Our faith embraces both of these concepts simultaneously, supporting the one without weakening the other.

It was the love of God that held Jesus to the Cross. There was no lack of power to save.

"Do you think that I cannot appeal to my Father, and he will at once send me more than twelve legions of angels?" (Matt. 26:53).

"No one takes it from me, but I lay it down of my own accord. I have authority to lay it down, and I have authority to take it up again. This charge I have received from my Father" (John 10:18).

Suffering Is Not a Sign of a Lack of Spirituality

David Brainerd (1718–1747) was a missionary to the Native Americans who had a very tumultuous life and died of tuberculosis at age 29. He was engaged to Jonathan Edward's daughter, but didn't live long enough to marry. He endured much external hardship including cold, hunger, and inadequate shelter. He experienced rejection and disillusionment. Worst of all were the nagging spiritual attacks and depression that haunted him. Consider the strong emotions he expressed in his journals.

December 16, 1744: Was so overwhelmed with dejection that I knew not how to live: I longed for death exceedingly: My soul was "sunk in deep waters," and "the floods" were ready to "drown me": I was so much oppressed that my soul was in a kind of horror.[1]

February 3, 1745: My soul remember "the wormwood and the gall" (I might almost say hell) of Friday last; and I was greatly afraid I should be obliged again to drink of that "cup of trembling," which was inconceivably more bitter than death, and made me long for the grave more, unspeakably more, than for hid treasures.[2]

Yet despite his great internal and external suffering, he found ways to turn his heart back to praise and gratitude.

February 21, 1746: My soul was refreshed and comforted, and I could not but bless God, who had enabled me in some good measure to be faithful in the day past. Oh, how sweet it is to be spent and worn out for God![3]

April 17, 1747: O I longed to fill the remaining moments all for God! Though my body was so feeble, and wearied with preaching and much private conversation, yet I wanted to sit up all night to do something for God. To God the giver of these refreshments, be glory forever and ever; Amen.[4]

By God's divine grace, Brainerd was able to call his suffering a "pleasing pain," because he knew it was drawing him closer to God and reminding him of his eternal home.

When I really enjoy God, I feel my desires of him the more insatiable, and my thirstings after holiness the more unquenchable . . . Oh, for holiness! Oh, for more of God in my soul! Oh, this pleasing pain! It makes my soul press

---

1. *The Life of David Brainerd*, ed. Norman Pettit, *The Works of Jonathan Edwards*, Vol. 7 (New Haven, CN: Yale University Press, 1985), p. 278.
2. Ibid., p. 285.
3. Ibid., p. 366.
4. Ibid., p. 246.

after God . . . Oh, that I might not loiter on my heavenly journey![5]

Purpose and Meaning in Suffering

Life's greatest defeats often result in the greatest gains. My painful experiences as a child shaped the person I am today. I am more intentional in my desire to be a godly husband and father than I ever would have been without my background. I have also been able to understand, and minister to, people that I could not have without being a victim of abuse. I wouldn't want to go through it again, but I thank God for allowing me to experience it.

> Blessed be the God and Father of our Lord Jesus Christ, the Father of mercies and God of all comfort, who comforts us in all our affliction, so that we may be able to comfort those who are in any affliction, with the comfort with which we ourselves are comforted by God. For as we share abundantly in Christ's sufferings, so through Christ we share abundantly in comfort too (2 Cor. 1:3–5).

In the Cross, love was not expressed in a context free of anguish and sorrow, but rather love was demonstrated *through* them. It is because of the Cross we know that all pain and suffering ultimately serves a redemptive purpose. God never allows us to experience any hurt or grief that He does not intend to utilize for His glory and our ultimate good.

> But we have this treasure in jars of clay, to show that the surpassing power belongs to God and not to us. We are afflicted in every way, but not crushed; perplexed, but not driven to despair; persecuted, but not forsaken; struck down, but not destroyed; always carrying in the body the death of Jesus, so that the life of Jesus may also be manifested in our bodies. For we who live are always being given

---

5. Ibid., p. 186.

over to death for Jesus' sake, so that the life of Jesus also may be manifested in our mortal flesh. So death is at work in us, but life in you. . . . So we do not lose heart. Though our outer self is wasting away, our inner self is being renewed day by day. For this light momentary affliction is preparing for us an eternal weight of glory beyond all comparison, as we look not to the things that are seen but to the things that are unseen. For the things that are seen are transient, but the things that are unseen are eternal (2 Cor. 4:7–18)

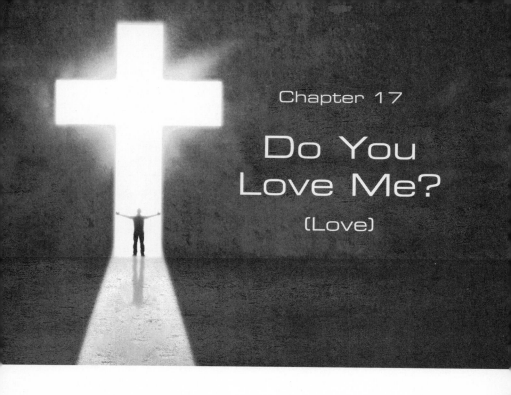

Chapter 17

Do You Love Me?

(Love)

I t is interesting to note that no other major religion in the world, outside of the Judeo/Christian tradition, promotes the concept of a loving God. In ancient mythologies, deities were more often malevolent tyrants to be feared, rather than gracious beings to be admired or adored. In Hinduism, the gods are often portrayed as half evil, and are not personal beings with whom you have a relationship. Buddhism promotes more of an impersonal force than a personal God. In Islam, Allah is to be feared and worshiped, but there is no concept of love as there is in the Christian faith.

What makes Christianity different? I believe it is largely because of the Incarnation. The New Testament teaches that God took the form of human flesh and lived among us in the life of Jesus Christ. Heaven came to earth, in a very real sense. It is this tangible expression of the deity that makes sense of the tragedy and suffering. God is not merely an austere master who lives out in the vast reaches of the universe, but He is near us, and even condescends to live in and through us.

Love and Service

J.C. Ryle (1816–1900), Anglican bishop of the church in Liverpool, England, in his sermon, "Do You Love Me?" shares this about loving Christ:

> Love to Christ is the mainspring of work for Christ. There is little done for His cause on earth from sense of duty, or from knowledge of what is right and proper. The heart must be interested before the hands will move and continue moving. Excitement may galvanize the Christian's hands into a fitful and spasmodic activity. But there will be no patient continuance in well–doing, no unwearied labor in missionary work at home or abroad, without love. The nurse in a hospital may do her duty properly and well, may give the sick man his medicine at the right time, may feed him, minister to him and attend to all his wants. But there is a vast difference between that nurse and a wife tending the sick–bed of a beloved husband, or a mother watching over a dying child. The one acts from a sense of duty; the other from affection and love. The one does her duty because she is paid for it; the other is what she is because of her heart. It is just the same in the matter of the service of Christ. The great workers of the church, the men who have led forlorn hopes in the mission–field, and turned the world upside down, have all been eminently lovers of Christ.
>
> Examine the characters of Owen and Baxter, of Rutherford and George Herbert, of Leighton and Hervey, of Whitefield and Wesley, of Henry Martyn and Judson, of Bickersteth and Simeon, of Hewitson and McCheyne, of Stowell and M'Neile. These men have left a mark on the world. And what was the common feature of their characters? They all loved Christ. They not only held a creed. They loved a Person, even the Lord Jesus Christ.[1]

---

1. www.SermonIndex.net.

Love and Betrayal

A significant answer to the question of evil in the world is the issue of love. Love can only truly exist in a world where people have the ability to choose love. Being forced to love against your will is the antithesis of real love. Because love is an inseparable part of God's being, He created a universe that would reflect His nature and character — a world of love.

As singer/songwriter Michael Card reminded us in a poignant lyric: "Only a friend could betray a friend. A stranger has nothing to gain. And only a friend comes close enough, to ever cause so much pain."[2]

Betrayal began, in the first cause, when Lucifer, a chief angel, rebelled against God. It continued in the first human family, when Cain murdered his innocent brother Abel. Throughout time and history, the tragic story of human treachery has been repeated over and over, reverberating like aftershocks from a cosmic relational earthquake.

Jesus, who became like us and experienced our humanity, was also the victim of betrayal. In the case of His chief antagonist, Judas, there was no opportunity for restoration. Judas tragically took his own life. However, there was a chance to restore fellowship and friendship with Peter. It is remarkable that Jesus did not wait for Peter to come to Him with an apology. I'm sure that would have been my inclination (if I could have forgiven him at all). Instead, Jesus pursued reconciliation with the man who had three times denied even knowing Him.

What Is Love?

In English, we often use the word *love* to cover an entire gamut of emotions and sentiments. We use the same word to say, "I love my wife and children" and "I love these potato chips." Our language has many limitations like this. The Greek language, in which the New

2. Roger Pulvers, Michael Card, Michael Lawrence Nyman, Embassy Music Corp. O/B/o Michael Nyman Ltd., Mole End Music

Testament was written, was far more diverse and precise in its ability to define specific meaning.

In ancient Greek, there were at least four words for love, two of which appear in the Bible.

The Biblical Terms

Agape (*agapao*): "In the New Testament, the fatherly love of God for humans and their reciprocal love for God. The term extends to the love of one's fellow humans" (Merriam Webster Dictionary).

Phileo: "From *philos*; to be a friend to (fond of [an individual or an object]), i.e., Have affection for (denoting personal attachment, as a matter of sentiment or feeling; while *agapao* is wider, embracing especially the judgment and the deliberate assent of the will as a matter of principle, duty and propriety" (Strong's Exhaustive Concordance, #5638).

The Non-Biblical Terms

Eros
1. "The Greek god of erotic love — compare cupid."
2. "The sum of life-preserving instincts that are manifested as impulses to gratify basic needs, as sublimated impulses, and as impulses to protect and preserve the body and mind" (Merriam Webster Dictionary).

Storge
1. "Natural or instinctual affection, as of a parent for a child" (Collins Dictionary).
2. In the conversation between Jesus and Peter, two distinct Greek words were used: *agape* and *phileo*.

Do You Love Me?

When they had finished breakfast, Jesus said to Simon Peter, "Simon, son of John, do you love [*agapao*] me more than these?" (John 21:15).

First, Jesus set an example for us as He met Peter's physical need (for food) before tending to his spiritual needs. Next He turned His focus to the business of reconciliation. Peter had been a braggadocio in his insistence that he would never deny Jesus, even if all the other disciples did (Matt. 26:35). He claimed to have a deeper love than the other disciples. Jesus wanted Simon to evaluate now, after having denied Jesus, how sincere his commitment really was.

It is interesting to note that Peter doesn't answer the question he is asked. Instead he uses a different word for love: *phileo*. It is the kind of affection held between brothers. It is from this word that we get our word for "Philadelphia" (the city of "brotherly love").

> He said to him, "Yes, Lord; you know [*oida*] that I love [*phileo*] you." He said to him, "Feed my lambs." He said to him a second time, "Simon, son of John, do you love [*agapao*] me?" (John 21:15–16).

> He said to him, "Yes, Lord; you know [*oida*] that I love [*phileo*] you." He said to him, "Tend my sheep." He said to him the third time, "Simon, son of John, do you love [*agapao*] me?" (John 21:16–17).

Jesus changes the question from, "Do you love me with a general Christian charity?" to "Do you truly love me as a friend?"

> Peter was grieved because he said to him the third time, "Do you love [*phileo*] me?" and he said to him, "Lord, you know everything; you know [*ginosko*] that I love [*phileo*] you." Jesus said to him, "Feed my sheep" (John 21:17).

Just as Jesus changes the word He uses for love in the third exchange, so Peter changes the word he uses for "know." *Oida*, the word most often used (at least 286 times) for "know" in the New Testament, means to understand something from seeing or general observation.

The second most frequently used word is *ginosko* (used 196 times in the New Testament). It implies knowledge that is born out of a more personal or intimate relationship with a person or situation.

It is as if Peter is at first saying, "Jesus, You can see that I love You." Then he changes and says, "Jesus, You know personally, from experience, that I love You."

Jesus had used this same approach with Peter when He washed his feet. "Jesus answered him, 'What I am doing you do not understand [*ouk oidas*] now, but afterward you will understand [*gnose*]' " (John 13:7). In other words, "What I am doing is not clear to you now from simple observation, but it will be clear to you later, through your personal experience of My service to you."

Jesus always led by example, never asking someone else to do a task that He was unwilling to perform Himself. When Peter was instructed to "feed my sheep," he knew what this looked like in a real-life context, because Jesus had done it for him personally. That is true discipleship.

Oswald Chambers (1874–1917) says:

> Peter now realizes that he does love Him, due to the revelation that came with the Lord's piercing question. The Lord's next point is — "Pour yourself out. Don't testify about how much you love Me and don't talk about the wonderful revelation you have had, just 'Feed My sheep.,' " Jesus has some extraordinarily peculiar sheep: some that are unkempt and dirty, some that are awkward or pushy, and some that have gone astray! But it is impossible to exhaust God's love, and it is impossible to exhaust my love if it flows from the Spirit of God within me.[3]

The call to Peter to be a "fisher of men" has come full circle to being invited to be a shepherd of sheep. It was around an evening fire with strangers that Peter denied the Lord. Here at the breakfast fire among friends, he finds himself restored.

---

3. Oswald Chambers, *My Utmost for His Highest*, http://utmost.org/his-commission-to-us.

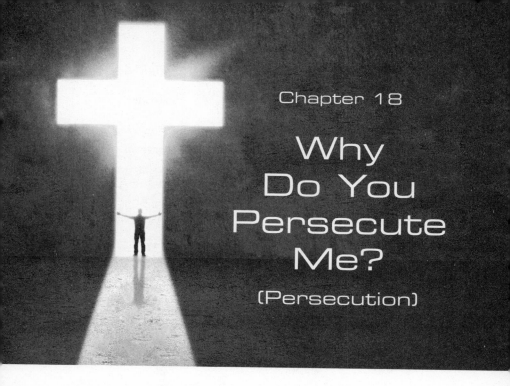

Chapter 18

Why Do You Persecute Me?

(Persecution)

I travel a lot, speaking at events around the country. One late night, I was driving hundreds of miles and was desperately seeking a way to stay awake, so I began to flip through the radio stations, hoping that an interesting discussion would keep me alert. I finally landed on a Christian call-in show for teenagers. The host picked the topic of religious persecution and asked the listeners if they had ever been persecuted because of their Christian faith. Most of the callers indicated they had experienced persecution, particularly in public school.

One young lady informed the host, "It's like, you know, like, some of my friends at school, you know, like, they don't want to hang around with me much, and stuff . . . because I'm a Christian." Others shared similar stories of fellow students snickering in biology class if they questioned evolution, or being laughed at by football teammates in the locker room if they hadn't crossed certain moral boundaries by the age of 15. Some admitted to having a hard time finding a date to go with them to the prom, because no one wanted to be with someone who "didn't believe in having fun."

While these situations certainly were serious and impactful to the young adults who experienced them, I had to ask myself if these personal slights and insults warranted the extreme title of "persecution."

The Blood of the Martyrs

Despite the relative ease we experience in the West to worship according to the dictates of our conscience, the fact remains that the majority of the world does not experience this freedom.

According to The Pew Research Center, over 75 percent of the world's population live in areas with severe religious restrictions. Many of these people are Christians. Also, according to the United States Department of State, Christians in more than 60 countries face persecution from their governments or surrounding neighbors simply because of their belief in the person of Jesus Christ.

I grew up being inspired by the stories of faithful Christians from generations past: *Foxe's Book of Martyrs, Martyr's Mirror, Tortured for Christ* by Richard Wurmbrand, *God's Smuggler* by Brother Andrew, and *The Hiding Place* by Corrie Ten Boom were all used greatly by God to open my eyes to the persecution of God's people around the world by those who oppose the gospel. All of these faithful and obedient servants make up that great cloud of witnesses that serve as our examples (see Heb. 12:1).

> I saw underneath the altar the souls of those who had been slain because of the word of God, and because of the testimony which they had maintained; and they cried out with a loud voice, saying, "How long, O Lord, holy and true, will You refrain from judging and avenging our blood on those who dwell on the earth?" And there was given to

each of them a white robe; and they were told that they should rest for a little while longer, until the number of their fellow servants and their brethren who were to be killed even as they had been, would be completed also (Rev. 6:9–11; NASB).

Ironically, persecution against the true, faithful, confessing Church has always caused it to grow (spiritually and numerically). This caused Tertullian (A.D. 160–225) to declare, "The blood of the martyrs is the seed of the Church."[1]

The Church's Worst Enemy

The first true villain in Church history was a guy named Saul from Tarsus. His dad had raised him in the strictest adherence to the Jewish sect called the Pharisees. He was very devout and committed to following God, as best as he understood devotion. He was present at the stoning of the first Christian martyr, Stephen.

Then they cast him out of the city and stoned him. And the witnesses laid down their garments at the feet of a young man named Saul (Acts 7:58).

Jesus foretold this very scenario:

"They will put you out of the synagogues. Indeed, the hour is coming when whoever kills you will think he is offering service to God. And they will do these things because they have not known the Father, nor me" (John 16:2–3).

Saul did not know Jesus. He knew about Jesus, but he didn't know Him properly. If Jesus were to ask Saul the question "Who do you say that I am?" I'm sure Saul would have said that Jesus was a misguided revolutionary, who tried to radicalize the Torah for His own personal interests. There was no way in a million

---

1. Tertullian, *Apologeticus*, Chapter 50.

that Saul would ever have viewed Jesus as the foretold Messiah, sent by God for the people of Israel. That wasn't part of Saul's worldview.

Saul was on a mission to arrest and persecute Jesus' followers wherever he could find them. It is ironic to me that some of the most virulent oppression against the Church through the ages has been at the hand of religious ideologues. But just as God has done with each of His children, Saul was engaged by a revelation of Jesus — in this case, on the road to Damascus.

> But Saul, still breathing threats and murder against the disciples of the Lord, went to the high priest and asked him for letters to the synagogues at Damascus, so that if he found any belonging to the Way, men or women, he might bring them bound to Jerusalem (Acts 9:1–2).

A Reluctant Convert

The Bible refers to some individuals as "enemies of the Cross" (see Phil. 3:18). Some people hate Christ and His gospel. It is hard for these people to admit their sin and guilt, humble themselves, and respond to God's grace. For some, the thought of becoming a Christian is the worst scenario they can imagine. Consider the hardened atheist Richard Dawkins becoming a Sunday school teacher! Many people have a strong antipathy toward anything that has to do with new life in Christ.

Nearly two millenniums after Saul's conversion, another reluctant convert, C.S. Lewis, described his encounter with the living Christ in a chapter entitled, "Checkmate":

> You must picture me alone in that room in Magdalen, night after night, feeling, whenever my mind lifted for even a second from my work, the steady, unrelenting approach of Him whom I so earnestly desired not to meet. That which I greatly feared had at last come upon me. In the Trinity

Term of 1929 I gave in, and admitted that God was God, and knelt and prayed: perhaps that night, the most dejected and reluctant convert in all England.[2]

Saul was the quintessential reluctant convert, but he was not too far gone to be reached by the long arm of the Lord.

> Now as he went on his way, he approached Damascus, and suddenly a light from heaven shone around him. And falling to the ground he heard a voice saying to him, "Saul, Saul, why are you persecuting me?" And he said, "Who are you, Lord?" And he said, "I am Jesus, whom you are persecuting. But rise and enter the city, and you will be told what you are to do" (Acts 9:3–6).

Why Are You Persecuting Me?

Do you notice that Jesus didn't ask Saul, "Why are you persecuting My people?" It seems at first glance that would have been a more appropriate question. We must remember that Jesus does not distance Himself from His people. He calls us His body here on earth (Eph. 5:30).

He said, "Truly, I say to you, as you did it to one of the least of these my brothers, you did it to me" (Matt. 25:40). From Jesus' point of view, persecuting one of His followers is the same as doing it to Him directly. Jesus assured us that, as disciples, life would not be a popularity contest.

> "Brother will betray brother to death, and a father his child; and children will rise up against parents and have them put to death. You will be hated by all because of My name, but the one who endures to the end, he will be saved" (Mark 13:12–13; NASB).

---

2. C.S. Lewis, *The Beloved Works: Surprised by Joy* (Edison, NJ: Inspirational Press, 2004), p. 125.

Blessed Are the Persecuted

The irony is that we are told by Jesus that we are "blessed" when we are persecuted.

> "Blessed and happy and enviably fortunate and spiritually prosperous (in the state in which the born-again child of God enjoys and finds satisfaction in God's favor and salvation, regardless of his outward conditions) are those who are persecuted for righteousness' sake (for being and doing right), for theirs is the kingdom of heaven! Blessed (happy, to be envied, and spiritually prosperous — with life-joy and satisfaction in God's favor and salvation, regardless of your outward conditions) are you when people revile you and persecute you and say all kinds of evil things against you falsely on My account" (Matt. 5:10–11, Amplified).

I remember once meeting a man from China who was part of the underground church there. I told him, "We are praying for the persecuted Church in China." He replied, "We are praying for the Church in America . . . that God would send you persecution!" I wasn't sure if I wanted to be on the receiving end of those "blessings." I rather like my ease, comfort, and security.

Despite our desire for peace and safety, the second-century Church Father Tertullian wrote, "The blood of martyrs is the seed of the Church,"[3] indicating the reality that the Church is always strengthened, deepened, and even ultimately expanded whenever it faces opposition.

Our rewards for faithful endurance are not in this life. Rather, we are striving for an eternal crown.

> Here is the perseverance of the saints who keep the commandments of God and their faith in Jesus. And I heard a voice from heaven, saying, "Write, 'Blessed are the dead who die in the Lord from now on!' " "Yes," says the

3. Tertullian, *Apologeticus*, chapter 50.

Spirit, "so that they may rest from their labors, for their deeds follow with them" (Rev. 14:12–13; NASB).

The Testimony of Polycarp

Polycarp was a student of the Apostle John and a defender of the faith against the emerging Gnosticism of his day. He lived about A.D. 69–155 in Smyrna, Turkey, and was an elder in the church there. Smyrna was the church to which Jesus said:

> "Do not fear what you are about to suffer. Behold, the devil is about to throw some of you into prison, that you may be tested, and for ten days you will have tribulation. Be faithful unto death, and I will give you the crown of life. He who has an ear, let him hear what the Spirit says to the churches. The one who conquers will not be hurt by the second death" (Rev. 2:10–11).

These prophetic words would come to pass within a generation when, as an old man, he was seized by a riotous mob, accused of being a Christian, and threatened with death. He was told by a sympathetic Roman proconsul that his life would be spared if he would just proclaim publicly his allegiance to Caesar as Lord.

Through the centuries, the powerful words of Polycarp have reverberated, "Eighty-six years have I served him," Polycarp declared, "and He has done me no wrong. How can I blaspheme my King and my Savior?"[4] He was burned at the stake for his testimony for Christ. He was one of the first of a faithful multitude who would overcome the world and devil: "And they have conquered him by the blood of the Lamb and by the word of their testimony, for they loved not their lives even unto death" (Rev. 12:11). May we each, if we are called upon, have the courage to take our stand for the One who gave everything for us! Blessed are the persecuted.

---

4. http://www.ccel.org/ccel/schaff/anf01.iv.iv.ix.html.

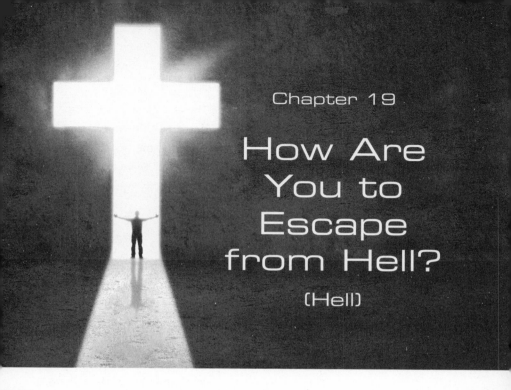

Chapter 19

How Are You to Escape from Hell?

(Hell)

E ven as a very young child, I had a close relationship with Christ and a passion for communicating with others about the gospel. When I was about four years old, some new neighbors moved in next door. They had a son and daughter who were close to the ages of my sister and me. My parents decided to invite them to our home for dinner to get to know them better.

It didn't take long for me to size up the situation and reach the definite conclusion that this family did not know God. My suspicions were confirmed at the dinner table when we bowed to give thanks for the food. I knew they couldn't possibly be Christians because they didn't close their eyes when they prayed! (Don't ask me how I knew that!) An awkward silence ensued after the prayer, as the adults were apparently at a loss regarding how to proceed. I was never at a loss! I may not have always been right, but I was never in doubt!

I decided to take the bull by the horns and get right down to the heart of the matter. I pointed my stubby little finger in the man's face and said as boldly as I could, "Mister! You're going to hell! And so is your wife, and so are your kids!"

There's nothing like a little direct hell-fire and brimstone preaching at the dinner table to really break the ice. My mother choked, stuffed a dinner roll in my mouth, and suddenly remembered something that was supposedly burning on the kitchen stove.

As I recall, for some reason, they moved shortly thereafter and we didn't see them again.

Did Jesus Believe in Hell?

Nearly everything we know about hell, we know from the teaching of Jesus. Ironic, isn't it? Our postmodern conception of Jesus is that He was a meek and mild teacher who taught tolerance and love, and would never judge anybody.

This popular belief, however, is far from what we find in the actions and teachings of the historical Jesus. He is the one who asked the scribes and the Pharisees, "You serpents, you brood of vipers, how are you to escape being sentenced to hell?" (Matt. 23:33).

Many mainline and evangelical churches have moved away from teaching on the doctrine of hell. It isn't terribly marketable at present. Some popular authors have suggested a kind of "universalism," where everyone makes it to paradise in the end, regardless of whether or not they have trusted in Jesus as their Lord and Savior. Their belief is that, because God is loving, "love wins" in the end (and triumphs over judgment).

However, Jesus would not be warning people to escape from something that didn't exist, and He wouldn't warn us if it were all up to fate and there was nothing that could be done to influence the outcome. Jesus was asking this question to religious leaders to get them to think about their future, and whether it was as hopeful and secure as they imagined (it was not!).

Let's look at a few popular myths regarding hell.

Universalism

> When the Son of Man comes in his glory, and all the angels with him, then he will sit on his glorious throne. Before him will be gathered all the nations, and he will separate people one from another as a shepherd separates the sheep from the goats. And he will place the sheep on his right, but the goats on the left. . . . Then he will say to those on his left, "Depart from me, you cursed, into the eternal fire prepared for the devil and his angels." . . . And these will go away into eternal punishment, but the righteous into eternal life (Matt. 25:31–46).

With this passage alone, I think it is safe to dismiss universalism. There is punishment, and it is eternal. There is an "in group" and an "out group." While this flies in the face of some people's concept of "fairness" and "equality," God gets to be the ultimate judge, not us.

There is also a myth that the God of the Old Testament was all wrath and doom, but the God of the New Testament is all about love and mercy. This dualism is a false dichotomy. God is the same yesterday, today, and forever (see Mal. 3:6; Heb. 13:8; James 1:17; Rev. 1:8). He has always been, and always will be, a perfect balance of grace, justice, and holiness.

> For if we go on sinning deliberately after receiving the knowledge of the truth, there no longer remains a sacrifice for sins, but a fearful expectation of judgment, and a fury of fire that will consume the adversaries. Anyone who has set aside the law of Moses dies without mercy on the evidence of two or three witnesses. How much worse punishment, do you think, will be deserved by the one who has trampled underfoot the Son of God, and has profaned the blood of the covenant by which he was sanctified, and has outraged the Spirit of grace? For we know him who said, "Vengeance is mine; I will repay." And again, "The Lord will judge his

people." It is a fearful thing to fall into the hands of the living God (Heb. 10:26–31).

Annihilationism

It is important to note that, according to Jesus, hell was never intended for humans. It was created for the devil and his angels. Bodies can die, but a spirit apparently can never be annihilated. Demons are fallen angels who will live forever. Yet, because of their rebellion against God, they cannot abide in God's presence because of His infinite holiness.

It has been said, "You are not a body who has a soul. You are a soul who has a body." It is this soul/spirit aspect of our being that will remain after death and, for Christians, receive a new body. That eternal soul of the human, like the created angels, cannot be destroyed and must live somewhere in eternity.

The Perpetual Party

British rockers AC/DC defiantly declared:

> Ain't nothin' that I'd rather do
> Goin' down
> Party time
> My friends are gonna be there too
> I'm on the highway to hell[1]

And someone said to him, "Lord, will those who are saved be few?" And he said to them, "Strive to enter through the narrow door. For many, I tell you, will seek to enter and will not be able. When once the master of the house has risen and shut the door, and you begin to stand outside and to knock at the door, saying, 'Lord, open to us,' then he will answer you, 'I do not know where you come from.' Then

---

1. Written by Angus Young, Malcolm Young, Bon Scott, © 1979 J Albert & Son Pty Ltd.

you will begin to say, 'We ate and drank in your presence, and you taught in our streets.' But he will say, 'I tell you, I do not know where you come from. Depart from me, all you workers of evil!' In that place there will be weeping and gnashing of teeth, when you see Abraham and Isaac and Jacob and all the prophets in the kingdom of God but you yourselves cast out" (Luke 13:23–28).

The eating and drinking will cease. Weeping and gnashing of teeth are sadly a far cry from the perpetual party that many envision.

Soul Sleep[2]

The Case for Soul Sleep

Here are a few verses people use to defend the concept that when we die, our souls go into a dormant, sleep-like state, only to be awakened at the end of the age:

And many of those who sleep in the dust of the earth shall awake, some to everlasting life, and some to shame and everlasting contempt (Dan. 12:2).

For the living know that they will die; but the dead know nothing, and they have no more reward, for the memory of them is forgotten (Eccles. 9:5).

And the dust returns to the earth as it was, and the spirit returns to God who gave it (Eccles. 12:7).

For David, after he had served the purpose of God in his own generation, fell asleep and was laid with his fathers and saw corruption (Acts 13:36).

Behold! I tell you a mystery. We shall not all sleep, but we shall all be changed (1 Cor. 15:51).

---

2. This doctrine is also referred to as "Christian Mortalism," "Psychopannychism," "Hypnopsychism," or "Thnetopsychism."

The Case against Soul Sleep

The best commentary on Scripture is always Scripture. Here are some other verses that demonstrate that, after a soul dies, it is not unaware.

> And he said, "Jesus, remember me when you come into your kingdom." And he said to him, "Truly, I say to you, today you will be with me in Paradise" (Luke 23:42–43).

The story of the rich man and Lazarus in Luke 16:19–31 demonstrates that there are souls who are experiencing paradise and suffering before the judgment.

At the transfiguration of Jesus in Matthew 17:1–8, we see Moses and Elijah, whose souls are not asleep. Elijah was taken and Moses clearly died (Deut. 34:5).

> When he opened the fifth seal, I saw under the altar the souls of those who had been slain for the word of God and for the witness they had borne. They cried out with a loud voice, "O Sovereign Lord, holy and true, how long before you will judge and avenge our blood on those who dwell on the earth?" (Rev. 6:9–10). (John sees these souls again in Rev. 20:4.)

I think the definitive passage, however, is found in 2 Corinthians 5:6–9, where Paul says, "So we are always of good courage. We know that while we are at home in the body we are away from the Lord, for we walk by faith, not by sight. Yes, we are of good courage, and we would rather be away from the body and at home with the Lord. So whether we are at home or away, we make it our aim to please him."

A Tour of Hell

In the 14th century, Dante Alighieri wrote *Inferno* as the opening to his epic poem *Divine Comedy*. He depicted nine circles of hell. The Bible, while not describing anything nearly so elaborate, does demonstrate some distinction of terms related to the afterlife.

Purgatory

Purgatory is not as much a place as it is a state. It contains the idea that God gives you a chance to have minor sins worked out and atoned for in the afterlife. Through the prayers of the living (and at least at one point in history, church donations), your spiritual sentence can be lightened.

From the *Cathechism of the Catholic Church*:

> All who die in God's grace and friendship, but still imperfectly purified, are indeed assured of their eternal salvation; but after death they undergo purification, so as to achieve the holiness necessary to enter the joy of heaven. The Church gives the name Purgatory to this final purification of the elect, which is entirely different from the punishment of the damned. The Church formulated her doctrine of faith on Purgatory especially at the Councils of Florence and Trent.[3]

Much could be said here but, for brevity's sake, I'm going to be a good little evangelical here and simply declare that, despite the teachings of the Catholic (and Eastern Orthodox) church on this issue, neither the term, nor the concept, of Purgatory show up anywhere in the Bible. Simple as that. It's an extra-biblical doctrine invented by men.

> And just as it is appointed for man to die once, and after that comes judgment (Heb. 9:27).

> For we must all appear before the judgment seat of Christ, so that each of us may receive what is due us for the things done *while in the body*, whether good or bad (2 Cor. 5:10; NIV, emphasis added).

Sheol

Throughout the Old Testament, we see the term *sheol*, describing the place where someone would go after death. Basically, the term

---

3. *Cathecism of the Catholic Church*, Part One, Section Two, Chapter Three, Article Twelve, III. The Final Purification or Purgatory, 1030–1032.

simply refers to "the grave," or the "place of the dead." It does not refer to a place of torment, but simply a place in the ground where your body was buried.

In the New Testament, the Bible seems to indicate that this "place of the dead" contains two holding places for souls awaiting judgment:

1. Paradise or Abraham's Bosom
2. Hades (a place of torment)

These places are not the final destiny of the soul. Eternal souls, after the judgment, will be sent into Gehenna (the lake of fire, or the Abyss or the "bottomless pit") or the New Jerusalem (the City of God), that comes down out of heaven (see Rev. 21:2).

Hades

Hades, a Greek word, comes out of ancient Greek mythology, and is the name for the god of the underworld. It corresponds closely to the Hebrew concept contained in sheol. In Acts 2:27, Luke translates the Hebrew term *sheol*, in Psalm 16:10 to *hades*: "you will not abandon my soul to Hades."

The passages that use this term are Matthew 11:23, 16:18; Luke 10:15, 16:23; Acts 2:27, 31; 1 Corinthians 15:551; and Revelation 1:18, 6:8, 20:13–14.

The rich man, who was being tormented in the story contained in Luke 16:23, is said to be in hades.

Gehenna

When the Bible speaks about the "Lake of Fire" and fiery torment, it is usually using the Greek word *Gehenna*.

In Jesus' day, the infamous city refuse dump was "ge-hinnom," or the "Valley of Hinnom," southwest of Jerusalem. This place was once called "Topheth" and derived from an Aramaic word meaning "fireplace." In the Old Testament, pagan kings had practiced human sacrifice at this location, burning their victims by fire (2 Chron. 28:3, 33:6; Jer. 7:31, 32:35).

Jesus is the only person in the New Testament who used this term, and He mentioned it 12 times. The ever-smoldering stench of the place gave the perfect word-picture for Jesus' audience of what eternal suffering would be like. If there was ever a hell on earth, Gehenna was it, and Jesus tapped into that imagery to make it real for His listeners. The passages that use this term are: Matthew 5:22, 29–30, 10:28, 18:9, 23:15, 33; Mark 9:43, 45, 47; Luke 12:5; and James 3:6.

Tartarus (Latin, from the Greek: Tartaroo or Tartaros)

This word appears only once in the Bible:

> For if God did not spare angels when they sinned, but cast them into hell [tataros] and committed them to chains of gloomy darkness to be kept until the judgment (2 Pet. 2:4).

In ancient Greek mythology, this name was "originally used for the deepest region of the world, the lower of the two parts of the underworld, where the gods locked up their enemies. It gradually came to mean the entire underworld. As such it was the opposite of Elysium, where happy souls lived after death."[4]

In ancient literature, it was initially underneath hades, but it seems that ancient Greek writers later used this word interchangeably with hades.

In the *Aeneid*, written by the Roman poet Virgil, between 29 and 19 B.C., Tartarus is described as "a gigantic place, the deepest part of the underworld, surrounded by the flaming river Phlegethon and triple walls to prevent its tormented captives from escaping."[5]

Hell Is Real

It seems that nearly every ancient culture had myths and legends about hell. Just as they have stories of gods, demons, epic floods,

---

4. Encyclopædia Britannica Online, s. v. "Tartarus", accessed November 17, 2014, http://www.britannica.com/EBchecked/topic/583773/Tartarus.
5. Virgil, *The Aeneid*, Bk VI:535-627, The Sibyl Describes Tartarus, quoted from: http://www.theopedia.com/Tartarus.

and other stories that are contained in the Bible, I believe even pagan cultures retained a memory of old narratives that were handed down from generation to generation since the time our common ancestors parted ways at the Tower of Babel.

Not only do nearly all cultures have stories about hell, I believe we also have eternity written on our hearts (see Eccles. 3:11). We know in our conscience that we are accountable to someone higher than ourselves.

Leonard Ravenhill (1907–1994) in his book *Why Revival Tarries,* recounts the last moments of the life of Charlie Peace, the notorious thief and murderer from Sheffield, England:

> He was taken on the death-walk. Before him went the prison chaplain, routinely and sleepily reading some Bible verses. The criminal touched the preacher and asked what he was reading. *The Consolations of Religion*, was the reply.
>
> Charlie Peace was shocked at the way he professionally read about hell. Could a man be so unmoved under the very shadow of the scaffold as to lead a fellow-human there and yet, dry-eyed, read of a pit that has no bottom into which this fellow must fall? Could this preacher believe the words that there is an eternal fire that never consumes its victims, and yet slide over the phrase without a tremor? Is a man human at all who can say with no tears, "You will be eternally dying and yet never know the relief that death brings"?
>
> All this was too much for Charlie Peace. "Sir," he addressed the preacher, "if I believed what you and the church of God say that you believe, even if England were covered with broken glass from coast to coast, I would walk over it, if need be, on hands and knees and think it worth while living, just to save one soul from an eternal hell like that!"[6]

6. Leonard Ravenhill, *Why Revival Tarries* (Bloomington, MN: Bethany House Publisher, 1959, 1987), p. 33–34.

Hell-Fire Preaching

While contemporary preachers avoid speaking on hell at all costs, the Puritans had no qualms about reminding their hearers of impending judgment. Jonathan Edwards' famous sermon, "Sinners in the Hands of an Angry God," was greatly used by God to convict souls of their eternal fate and ignite the First Great Awakening:

> There is the dreadful pit of the glowing flames of the wrath of God; there is hell's wide gaping mouth open; and you have nothing to stand upon, not any thing to take hold of. There is nothing between you and hell but the air; 'tis only the power and mere pleasure of God that holds you up. You probably are not sensible of this; you find you are kept out of hell, but don't see the hand of God in it, but look at other things, as the good state of your bodily constitution, your care of your own life, and the means you use for your own preservation. But indeed these things are nothing; if God should withdraw his hand; they would avail not more to keep you from falling than the thin air to hold up a person that it is suspended in it. Your wickedness makes you as it were heavy as lead, and to tend downwards with great weight and pressure towards hell; and if God should let you go, you would immediately sink and swiftly descend and plunge into the bottomless gulf.

As sinners heard about their future eternal fate, many fell to their knees under the weight of a holy fear and cried out to God to save them. They desperately wanted to receive the favor and mercy of God on this side of the judgment, rather than stand before a Holy God and be condemned.

The Great White Throne Judgment

> And the devil who had deceived them was thrown into the lake of fire and sulfur where the beast and the false

prophet were, and they will be tormented day and night forever and ever. Then I saw a great white throne and him who was seated on it. From his presence earth and sky fled away, and no place was found for them. And I saw the dead, great and small, standing before the throne, and books were opened. Then another book was opened, which is the book of life. And the dead were judged by what was written in the books, according to what they had done. And the sea gave up the dead who were in it, Death and Hades gave up the dead who were in them, and they were judged, each one of them, according to what they had done. Then Death and Hades were thrown into the lake of fire. This is the second death, the lake of fire. And if anyone's name was not found written in the book of life, he was thrown into the lake of fire (Rev. 20:10–15).

Jesus spoke more about hell than anyone else in the Bible because He, more than anyone else, wanted to warn you to flee from it. The question Jesus is asking you today is, "How are you to escape being sentenced to hell?" The only escape available to you is to trust in Jesus to save you.

For God so loved the world, that he gave his only Son, that whoever believes in him should not perish but have eternal life. For God did not send his Son into the world to condemn the world, but in order that the world might be saved through him. Whoever believes in him is not condemned, but whoever does not believe is condemned already, because he has not believed in the name of the only Son of God (John 3:16–18).

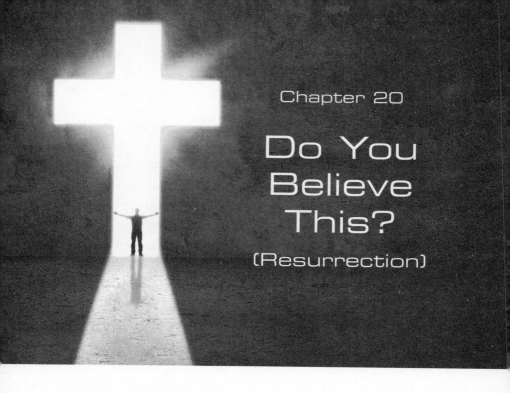

Chapter 20

Do You Believe This?

(Resurrection)

Not long ago, my friend Rachel died. Her heart stopped beating, and she fell and hit her head on the pavement. The medics arrived and declared her dead. She was only 31 years old. When things like that happen to someone so young, who had been healthy up to that point, it leaves you feeling confused, shaken, and vulnerable. Rachel had a lot of life ahead of her. She still had things to do. Her friends weren't ready to see her go. But death is often sudden, and always final . . . except in Rachel's case.

Rachel is doing great now and enjoying her second shot at life. Rachel's heart had stopped beating for 12 minutes, as medics worked frantically to bring her back from the other side. Fortunately for all of us, God sovereignly decided to allow their efforts to be efficacious, and Rachel has been granted the ability to pursue some more dreams before her final day arrives.

I joked with Rachel that she now has ultimate bragging rights in any story competition. No matter what I try, I don't think I'll be able to match up. "Rachel, did I ever tell you about the time I fell out of a tree and landed on my head?" To which I'm sure she'll reply, "No, I don't think so . . . but did I ever tell you about the time I *died*?!" Seriously, who can top that?

I tend to think that once you have died, it would radically change your perspective on living. Unfortunately for Rachel, who is a writer, she didn't have any out-of-body experiences or visions of heaven to help her land on the *New York Times* bestseller list. However, she does have the personal knowledge that everything could have ended right there, had her heart not started beating again.

Death is something none of us want to think about, but it is something that all of us must face.

The Death of Lazarus

Jesus had some very good friends — Martha, Mary, and Lazarus — who lived in the town of Bethany. Jesus loved them and enjoyed spending time in their home. One day when Jesus was out of town, word came to Him from Mary and Martha that Lazarus was ill. You would think that Jesus, who had the power to heal the sick, would have raced as fast as He could to make sure that Lazarus didn't die.

No, that wasn't Jesus' plan. Much to the surprise of His disciples, Jesus waited until His friend died. By the time He finally left for Bethany, Lazarus had been dead for four days. Martha heard that Jesus was on His way and met Him about two miles outside of town.

> Martha said to Jesus, "Lord, if you had been here, my brother would not have died. But even now I know that whatever you ask from God, God will give you." Jesus said to her, "Your brother will rise again." Martha said to him, "I know that he will rise again in the resurrection on the last day." Jesus said to her, "I am the resurrection and the life. Whoever believes in me, though he die, yet shall he live, and everyone who lives and believes in me shall never die. Do you believe this?" (John 11:21–26).

Jesus Questions Martha

Perhaps you have been tempted, as I have, to think of Martha as being somewhat faithless in this exchange. Rather than immediately embracing the idea that her brother, who had been dead for four days and now "stinketh" (in the words of the KJV), would leap back to life, she turns her focus to her hope in the future resurrection of all of the faithful God-followers.

If you look closely at the text, however, Jesus doesn't scold her for this answer. Instead, He actually reaffirms it. He declares that everyone who lives and believes in Him will never die. This statement is not limited to her brother. It extends to all true believers. Jesus reaffirms her belief in His power, not merely over the death of Lazarus, but instead, He declares His triumph over death itself! Then He asks her, "Do you believe this?"

She replied with the equivalent of a blank check of faith: "Yes, Lord; I believe that you are the Christ, the Son of God, who is coming into the world" (John 11:27). Whatever Jesus says, whatever Jesus intends, Martha is willing to trust His power and His goodness, even in the face of the death of her brother! The greater miracle is not the healing of sickness, but rather of sin. It is not the healing of this earthly body, but the promise of an immortal one.

T. Austin Sparks (1888–1971) talks about this ultimate healing that Jesus promises to all who believe:

> Perhaps some of you have heard of God's great servant, Dr. A.B. Simpson (1843–1919). He was a great believer in divine healing and wrote a book on it. But, in spite of his belief, he said this: "So that no one will misunderstand my position, I do not say that everyone has to be healed, but I do say that everyone can know divine life, which is something more than natural life." Well, back to Lazarus. The Lord did not heal him, but He gave him resurrection life, and that is the hope of everyone. The Lord may want to heal you in your body, or He may not do it. However, whether

He does or does not, He does not want us to live on our own life, but by resurrection life. That is what Jesus meant when He said: "This sickness is not unto death, but for the glory of God" [John 11:4; KJV]. If you look through your New Testament you will see that God is always glorified in resurrection. That is where the glory of God is.[1]

The Resurrection of Jesus

The hope of the final resurrection of the dead (some to judgment and eternal fire, and the righteous to eternal life) is central to the story of the Bible. Every narrative finds its root in *the* meta-narrative (the big story of all time). Every good story ultimately has a happy ending. That is because we sense intuitively that everything is supposed to resolve. As Christians, our eschatology (our view of final things) is a hopeful one, because we believe that all the wrongs will be put right in the end. There will be a restoration of all things. All of this is made possible because of the final and complete defeat of death by Jesus on the Cross, and His subsequent Resurrection.

Some contemporary scholars try to dismiss the bodily Resurrection of Jesus as being irrelevant or untrue, but the Apostle Paul allows for no such theories. He says that the story of the death, burial, and Resurrection of Jesus are of "first importance"!

Now I would remind you, brothers, of the gospel I preached to you, which you received, in which you stand, and by which you are being saved, if you hold fast to the word I preached to you — unless you believed in vain. For I delivered to you as of first importance what I also received: that Christ died for our sins in accordance with the Scriptures, that he was buried, that he was raised on the third day in accordance with the Scriptures, and that he appeared to

1. T. Austin Sparks (in the sermon, "The Glory of God in Resurrection"), www. SermonIndex.net.

Cephas, then to the twelve. Then he appeared to more than five hundred brothers at one time, most of whom are still alive, though some have fallen asleep. Then he appeared to James, then to all the apostles. Last of all, as to one untimely born, he appeared also to me (1 Cor. 15:1–8).

Jesus' Resurrection has tremendous implications for our future. Because He lives, we too will live. Paul taught that if this doctrine of Jesus' Resurrection wasn't true, we are in a heap of eternal trouble! Tertullian (A.D. 160–220) declared, "The resurrection of the dead is the Christian's trust. By it we are believers."[2]

Now if Christ is proclaimed as raised from the dead, how can some of you say that there is no resurrection of the dead? But if there is no resurrection of the dead, then not even Christ has been raised. And if Christ has not been raised, then our preaching is in vain and your faith is in vain. We are even found to be misrepresenting God, because we testified about God that he raised Christ, whom he did not raise if it is true that the dead are not raised. For if the dead are not raised, not even Christ has been raised. And if Christ has not been raised, your faith is futile and you are still in your sins. Then those also who have fallen asleep in Christ have perished. If in Christ we have hope in this life only, we are of all people most to be pitied. But in fact Christ has been raised from the dead, the firstfruits of those who have fallen asleep. For as by a man came death, by a man has come also the resurrection of the dead. For as in Adam all die, so also in Christ shall all be made alive (1 Cor. 15:12–22).

---

2. Quintus Septimius Florens Tertullianus, translated by Peter Holmes, from *Ante-Nicene Fathers*, Vol. 3, edited by Alexander Roberts, James Donaldson, and A. Cleveland Coxe (Buffalo, NY: Christian Literature Publishing Co., 1885). Revised and edited for New Advent by Kevin Knight. <http://www.newadvent.org/fathers/0316.htm>.

Who Are Your Looking For?

It is fascinating to me that as often as Jesus prophesied His death and Resurrection, those closest to Him still didn't seem to connect the dots.

The angels asked the women who came to anoint the dead body of Jesus, "Why do you seek the living among the dead?" (Luke 24:5). Who were they looking for? A dead messiah? What good is that kind of savior?

When Mary Magdalene arrived at the tomb, looking for Jesus' lifeless corpse, she was approached and questioned by the angels, and then by the Lord Himself.

> But Mary stood weeping outside the tomb, and as she wept she stooped to look into the tomb. And she saw two angels in white, sitting where the body of Jesus had lain, one at the head and one at the feet. They said to her, "Woman, why are you weeping?" She said to them, "They have taken away my Lord, and I do not know where they have laid him." Having said this, she turned around and saw Jesus standing, but she did not know that it was Jesus. Jesus said to her, "Woman, why are you weeping? Whom are you seeking?" (John 20:11–15).

Why did Jesus ask these questions? What was He trying to get Mary to stop and consider? What were her assumptions? What was she believing about Jesus, His promises, and His future? What was her relationship with Him to be like from now on? Was she content to merely anoint a decaying body? Was she content to live with her memories of the past, or did she have faith about the future?

> Supposing him to be the gardener, she said to him, "Sir, if you have carried him away, tell me where you have laid him, and I will take him away." Jesus said to her, "Mary." She turned and said to him in Aramaic, "Rabboni!" (which means Teacher). Jesus said to her, "Do not cling to me, for I

have not yet ascended to the Father; but go to my brothers and say to them, "I am ascending to my Father and your Father, to my God and your God." Mary Magdalene went and announced to the disciples, "I have seen the Lord" — and that he had said these things to her (John 20:15–18).

Evidence for the Resurrection of Jesus

What historical evidence is there that Jesus actually rose from the dead? Is this just a conspiracy started by Jesus' followers, who didn't want to admit that their movement was over?

In his book *The New Evidence that Demands a Verdict*, Christian apologist Josh McDowell outlines the following argument for the Resurrection of Jesus:

> There are only two explanations for the empty tomb:
> 1. Human work
>   Removed by Enemies — No Motive
>   Removed by Friends — No Power
> 2. A Divine Work (the most logical conclusion)[3]

The Apostles were neither deceived nor deceivers. Not only did the Apostles declare that they were eyewitnesses of Jesus' bodily Resurrection, according to church tradition, but all of them were brutally killed clinging to this profession. People will occasionally go to the death for something they believe to be true, but no one will willingly face torture and death for something they know is a lie they invented.

Dr. Henry Morris (1918-2006), founder of the Institute for Creation Research, outlines the post-mortem appearances of Jesus:

> The Appearances of Christ
>   Not only was the tomb empty, but the disciples actually saw their resurrected Lord on at least ten separate occasions

---

3. Josh McDowell, *The New Evidence that Demands a Verdict* (Nashville, TN: Thomas Nelson Publishers, 1999), p. 264.

after He left the tomb. These appearances were probably in the following order:

1. To Mary Magdalene (John 20:11–18; Mark 16:9)

2. To the other women (Matthew 28:8–10)

3. To Peter (Luke 24:34; 1 Corinthians 15:5)

4. To the two on the road to Emmaus (Luke 24:13–35; Mark 16:12)

5. To 10 of the disciples (Luke 24:36–43; John 20:19–29)

6. To all 11 disciples, eight days later (John 20:24–29)

7. To 7 disciples by the Sea of Tiberias (John 21:1–23)

8. To five hundred followers (1 Corinthians 15:6)

9. To James (1 Corinthians 15:7)

10. To the 11, at the ascension (Acts 1:3–12)[4]

Testimony of the Early Church

All four of the gospel narratives, Acts, the 13 epistles of Paul, 1 John, 1 Peter, and Revelation all affirm the Resurrection of Jesus. It was accepted by early Christian writers such as Athenagoras, Justin Martyr, Ignatius, Origen, Clement of Rome (in his epistle to the Corinthians in A.D. 95), Polycarp (in his epistle to the Philippians in A.D. 110), Irenaeus, Cyprian, Tertullian, and all of the early Christian creeds, and even non-Christian sources like Josephus make reference to the wide-spread account of His Resurrection (in A.D. 93–94).[5]

There is no doubt that something extraordinary happened on that third day after the death of Jesus. It turned the entire history of

---

4. Henry Morris, *Many Infallible Proofs* (San Diego, CA: Master Books, 1978), p. 381, www.icr.org/ChristResurrection.

5. Flavius Josephus, "Testimonium Flavianum," *The Works of Flavius Josephus, Antiquities of the Jews*, Book 18, Chapter 3, Section 3.

the world, and even historical time itself hinges on the life of Jesus of Nazareth. The disciples went from being a rather dysfunctional band of narcissists and misfits to a cohesive unit whose enemies accused them of having "turned the world upside down" (Acts 17:6).

There is far more historical evidence for Christ's Resurrection and, for this, I point you to the writings of Josh McDowell, William Lane Craig, Gary Habermas, and others.

Do You Believe This?

Jesus' question stands before each of us. Do you believe that life and death are ultimately in His hands? Do you believe that He has defeated sin and death and hell and has provided eternal life for each of us? Do you believe He is the resurrection and the life, and those who believe in Him will never face eternal death? Do you trust Him to be Lord over everything in this life and in the life to come? Do you believe this?

Appendix I — Hypostatic Union

Theologians have long explored the two natures of Jesus: His divinity and His humanity. In theology proper, this concept is called the hypostatic union.

Over the centuries, a number of heresies have arisen because of an imbalanced focus on the humanity of Christ, minimizing His deity, or in some cases, focusing so exclusively on His divinity, that His humanness is undermined.[1]

One of the errors some have embraced is believing that Jesus could not have truly been God, and died to pay the penalty for our sins, because God cannot die. Another is that Jesus was a spiritual being, and could not (or did not) live in a physical body.

Christian doctrine insists that Jesus is fully God and fully man, and never does the one minimize or negate the other.

Jesus Was with God, and Jesus Was God

While Jesus lived 33 years as God in the body of a human male, He lived as a co-equal part of the tri-unity of God for all eternity. In John 17:5, Jesus claimed to be pre-existent with God, "And now, Father, glorify me in your own presence with the glory that I had with you before the world existed." He also said in John 3:13: "No one has ascended into heaven except he who descended from heaven, the Son of Man."

Unlike the teachings of some cults, people are not pre-existent spirits waiting up in heaven to be accepted by a human body so they can be born on earth. Jesus' claim to be with the Father before the world was created, can only be made by an uncreated, co-eternal member of the Godhead.

---

1. For a more detailed analysis of the ancient heresies that resulted from an imperfect view of the hypostatic union, please refer to an article by Troy Lacey entitled "The Hypostatic Union," https://answersingenesis.org/jesus-christ/incarnation/the-hypostatic-union/.

Jesus as God	Jesus as Man
He is worshiped (Matt. 2:2, 11, 14:33)	He worshiped the Father (John 17)
He is prayed to (Acts 7:59)	He prayed to the Father (John 17)
He is sinless (1 Pet. 2:22; Heb. 4:15)	He was tempted (Matt. 4:1)
He knows all things (John 21:17)	He grew in wisdom (Luke 2:52)
He gives eternal life (John 10:28)	He died (Rom. 5:8)
All the fullness of the deity dwells in Him (Col. 2:9)	He has a body of flesh and bones (Luke 24:39)

In Matthew 28:20, Jesus claimed both eternality and omnipresence: ". . . teaching them to observe all that I have commanded you. And behold, I am with you always, to the end of the age." It is obvious that a finite being cannot be with someone, everywhere they go, on an infinite basis. Jesus was speaking beyond the scope of His earthly life span. He is referring here to His divinity, not His humanity.[2]

---

2. The comparison lists of "Jesus as God" and "Jesus as Man" were compiled by Matt Slick at CARM.org.

Appendix II — The Communicato Idiomatum

Closely related to the doctrine of the hypostatic union is the *communicato idiomatum,* which is Latin, meaning "communication of properties." It discusses which attributes of God are innate to His being, and cannot be transferred to anyone who is not God, versus those that can be, and are, transmitted to created beings.

The Communicable Attributes of God

There are many of God's qualities that He graciously imparts and imputes to us. The fruits of the Spirit in Galatians 5:22–23 come to mind: love, joy, peace, patience, kindness, goodness, faithfulness, gentleness, and self-control. Not only are those things part of the nature and character of God, but they also can be transferred to us through the infilling and empowering of the Holy Spirit. As beings, made in His image, we share many characteristics with our Creator.

The Incommunicable Attributes of God

However, there are other attributes that belong to God alone, and cannot be transferred to another: God's omniscience (all-knowing), omnipresence (present everywhere at once), omnipotence (all-powerful) and eternality (God was never created, but has always existed, and because God cannot die, always will exist).

When we look at the hypostatic union (see the other appendix), one question we must ask ourselves is this: "Did Jesus possess the incommunicable attributes of God during His incarnate state (when He lived in a physical body on earth)?"

The Fullness of God

When the Bible speaks of the fullness of God dwelling in Jesus, it is speaking of the communicable attributes of God:

> For in him all the fullness of God was pleased to dwell (Col. 1:19).

> For in him the whole fullness of deity dwells bodily (Col. 2:9).

In the same way, when it talks about our experiencing the fullness of God, it certainly is not talking about the incommunicable attributes:

> And to know the love of Christ that surpasses knowledge, that you may be filled with all the fullness of God (Eph. 3:19).

The fullness of God lived bodily in Jesus (Col. 2:9). We are commanded to be full of the Spirit of God, who lives in us (Eph. 3:19). However, while the Spirit of God lives within us, we can only ever have the communicable attributes of God.

Jesus Laid Aside His Glory

I think it is safe to say that in His physical body, Jesus was not everywhere at once (omnipresent), nor was His earthly body eternal, though He is divine and eternal. The more difficult questions relate to His omnipotence (having all-power) and omniscience (being all-knowing). Was Jesus omnipotent in His humanity? Jesus appealed to having angels available to help Him, rather than taking authority over His enemies Himself: "Do you think that I cannot appeal to my Father, and he will at once send me more than twelve legions of angels?" (Matt. 26:53). However, it seems that He had some pretty extraordinary power, above and beyond what was evidenced even in the Apostles, by causing the wind and waves to be still (Mark 4:39). So if Jesus' power was in some way limited during His time on earth, it was clearly not that He didn't have access to the power, but rather that He voluntarily chose not to utilize it.

The same is true with the omniscience of Jesus (which is dealt with in the Introduction of this book). Some of Jesus' questions clearly demonstrate special knowledge, but they could have been attributed to possessing the fullness of the communicable attributes of God (being filled with the Spirit), as the Apostles also had special moments of knowing things they could not have otherwise (Acts 5:3). Other questions seem to indicate that He was using ordinary observation and human sensitivity, just as we do.

At any rate, whether His questions were rooted in omniscient knowledge, special revelation from the Spirit, or just human intuition, all of His questions probe the heart and motives of His hearers. His questions are recorded in the Bible for us as well. They challenge our preconceived notions and assumptions. They examine our values and desires. They help us to consider our relationship to God, and to our fellow man. Jesus' desire for us is that we will walk in the fullness of every attribute and characteristic of God that is possible. He gave us an example of living in close fellowship and communion with the Father, so that we can do the same (see John 14).

New Leaf Press

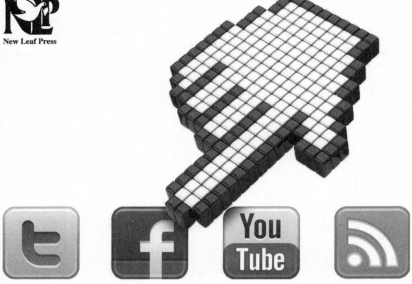

Connect with New Leaf Press®

newleafpress.net   An Imprint of New Leaf Publishing Group

facebook.com/**masterbooks**
twitter.com/**masterbooks4u**
youtube.com/**nlpgvideo**

nlpgblogs.com

join us at **Creation**Conversations.com
Connecting Christians who believe in Biblical Creation

To stay informed, receive event notifications,
discounts, and more, sign up for New Leaf
Publishing Group's e-newsletter here:
nlpg.com/newsletter/signup